Enlightened Living

RANGJUNG YESHE BOOKS

Padmasambhava
Advice from the Lotus-Born
Dakini Teachings (Shambhala Publ.)

Padmasambhava and Jamgön Kongtrül
Light of Wisdom, Vol I (Shambhala Publ.)

Yeshe Tsogyal
The Lotus-Born (Shambhala Publ.)

Gampopa
The Precious Garland of the Sublime Path

Tsele Natsok Rangdröl
The Heart of the Matter
Mirror of Mindfulness
Empowerment
Lamp of Mahamudra

Mipham Rinpoche
Gateway to Knowledge, Vol I

Tulku Urgyen Rinpoche
Rainbow Painting
Repeating the Words of the Buddha

Ten Lamas
In Memory of Kyabje Tulku Urgyen Rinpoche

Khenchen Thrangu Rinpoche
Songs of Naropa
King of Samadhi
Buddha Nature

Chökyi Nyima Rinpoche
Indisputable Truth
The Union of Mahamudra and Dzogchen
Song of Karmapa
Bardo Guidebook

Tulku Thondup
Enlightened Living

Orgyen Tobgyal Rinpoche
Life and Teachings of Chokgyur Lingpa

Enlightened Living

Teachings of Tibetan Buddhist Masters

Translated by
Tulku Thondup

Edited by
Harold Talbott

Rangjung Yeshe Publications
Hong Kong, Esby & Boudhanath
1997

Rangjung Yeshe Publications
125 Robinson Road, flat 6A
Hong Kong

Mailing Address:
Rangjung Yeshe Publications
Ka-Nying Shedrub Ling Monastery
P.O. Box 1200, Kathmandu, Nepal

9 8 7 6 5 4 3 2

First edition, 1990, Shambhala Publ., Boston
Second edition, 1997

Printed in the United States of America on recycled acid-free paper

A Buddhist Classic

Publication Data:

Enlightened Living: Teachings of Tibetan Buddhist Masters. Translated by Tulku Thondup. Edited by Harold Talbot.
2nd ed. Translated from Tibetan. Includes teachings by Patrul Rinpoche, Jigmed Thrinley Odzer, Lobzang Thubten Longtog Gyatsho, Jigmed Tenpai Nyima, and Rigdzin Jigmed Lingpa.
ISBN 962-7341-30-7
1. Spiritual life, Buddhism). 2. Buddhism—Tibet. I Thondup, Tulku. II Talbott, Harold.

"If I give this, what shall have left to enjoy?"
Such selfish thinking is the way of demons.
"If I enjoy this, what shall I have left to give?"
Such selfless thinking is a quality of the gods.

Foes are as unlimited as space,
They cannot possibly all be overcome;
Yet if you just overcome the thought of hatred,
That will be equal to overcoming all foes.

Where is the leather
With which one can cover the earth?
But wearing a leather sandal
Is equal to covering the earth with leather.

If a problem can be solved,
Why are you unhappy?
And if it cannot be solved,
What is the use of being unhappy?

—Śāntideva

Contents

Preface

This book includes translations of eight texts written by great Nyingmapa scholars of Tibet. Throughout the book I have added some synonyms in square brackets.

The titles of texts quoted are indicated by abbreviations, for example, *BP* means *Byang-Ch'ub Sems-dPa'i sPyod-Pa La 'Jug-Pa* (Sanskrit: *Bodhicaryāvatāra*) by Śāntideva. They are alphabetically listed in the Key to the Abbreviations of Works Cited. When a text is quoted, the letters signifying the title are followed by the folio number, then the letter "a" or "b" meaning the front or back side of the folio, and then the line number. For example, DN3a/3.

I have capitalized the root letters (*Ming-gZhi*) of each Tibetan word in the transliterated Tibetan in order to ensure a correct reading. When the root letters are not capitalized, it is possible to confuse two entirely different words. For example, *Gyi* means "of," while the meaning of *gYi* is "lynx."

Tulku Thondup
Cambridge, Mass.
1989

Acknowledgments

I am thankful to the following friends, whose compassionate and wise minds and skills have helped me in producing this book. The translations of texts number 1, 3, 4, 5, 6, 7, and 8 were edited by Harold Talbott. Paul Levine assisted in translating and editing text number 2. Steve Goodman revised the translation of text number 8 and arranged the Sanskrit words, mantras, and dhāraṇīs contained in the text. Lydia Segal encouraged me to put these texts together as a book and helped me to check the manuscript.

I am grateful to Michael Baldwin and the members and patrons of Buddhayana, U.S.A., under whose most kind and generous sponsorship I have been working on my academic projects for the past several years. I am sincerely thankful to Victor and Ruby Lam for providing a lovely apartment for me in which to live and work on my academic projects. My thanks also to Larry Mermelstein and Peter Turner of Shambhala Publications for their thorough scholarship and editorial skill; and to Brian Boland, also of Shambhala, for his work on the design of the book.

Introduction

This book includes translations of eight writings by famous Tibetan Buddhist masters. The main subjects are spiritual and secular ethics according to Tibetan culture and Buddhist tradition, and how to pursue day-to-day moral and spiritual life. Most Buddhist writings are generally on how to transcend the worldly realms and attain enlightenment, or Buddhahood. However, the writings included in this book are mainly teachings on how to live and behave in this world and serve society.

The main goal of the Mahāyāna Buddhist view and disciplines is to bring joy, peace, wisdom, and Buddhahood to all living beings. But Mahāyānists also believe that in order to serve others it is important to improve and perfect one's own spiritual strength. A person who is a worshiper of ego, drunk with emotions and glued to so-called political and social principles, interests, and associations, will hardly be able to help others in the true sense. Instead of helping others, such a person may be spreading negative influences, like charcoal that makes everything dirty by contact, even if it is in an artistic design, or like a garbage bag emitting a stink just by being around, even if it is in a colorful container. Such a person could hardly provide any spiritual or true support to people with problems. It would be like relying on the shoulder of a falling person. According to Buddhism, in order to improve oneself, first one has to discipline one's mental character and attitude, as the mind is the main element and the forerunner of all activities. In the *Dharmapada* the Buddha[1] said:

> Mind is the main element and the forerunner of all.
> If with a hateful mind
> One speaks or acts,
> He suffers because of that
> Just as the wheel of the cart follows the horse.

If one's spiritual or mental attitude is improved and perfected, then whatever one says or does, it will be out of a peaceful, wise, and pure mind, and this brings true, enduring joy and peace to others. Even the mere presence of a person of peace, joy, and wisdom enlightens the surroundings, and so a little effort could make a great and pure support for others.

At the same time, for people like us who are slaves of objective phenomena, the physical disciplines are an important factor in inspiring and improving our mental attitude; but still the goal of physical discipline is the mind, and this should never be overlooked.

We ordinary people are slaves of dualistic perception, intellectual apprehensions, emotional passion, and the lordship of objects. Whatever views and values we have are formed under the influence of those adventitious forces. Through your spiritual meditative trainings, you will become free from the slavery of external forces and adventitious emotions and will reach your inner peace, free from adventitious concepts and emotions. When you have attained such a state, remaining in that balanced center of peace and omniscience, you can see and deal with the world that appears before you in a simple, easy, and perfect way. If you are free from the effects of other forces, and if you are poised with utmost peace and positive energies, then phenomenal objects appear vividly before you and you will perceive them clearly as they are, without emotional taint and habitual bias. In *The Power of Myth,* Joseph Campbell writes: "There's a center of quietness within, which has to be known and held. If you lose that center, you are in tension and begin to fall." In any field of life and with any kind of success, it is important to find and remain in one's own inner balanced and peaceful center. For example, for athletes like figure skaters and ballet dancers the important thing is to find and rely on their self, a center within. If they can find and remain in it, then they can perform much more easily, but if they lose that center, self, or balanced feeling and position they will fail to do well. This illustration is about a simple part of life, but in the spiritual process the principle is the same. The main focus of spiritual training is to find the peace within. If you can find in yourself a center, a peaceful, blissful, balanced, and independent state, and if you remain in it, then you can deal with life's happenings on your own terms. Otherwise, if you are overwhelmed by other people, then as a slave you will think, feel, and live under the terms of others, and you will go through various experiences generated by and soaked in emotions, the creation of dualistic concepts depending upon others.

So, to discipline your mental attitude and also to dedicate yourself to physical activities that inspire the virtues of the mind, and then finally to dedicate your whole life to the service of others with the strength of peace, joy, tolerance, and wisdom is the way of Buddhist discipline. However, even if your mental strength is not perfect, if there are services that you can perform for society, you should dedicate yourself to such activities with the proper attitude, with fewer emotional attachments or none at all.

Even if you have no so-called religious inclination, if you pursue any behavior that brings true or at least partial peace and joy to society or your own life, that is a discipline in the Path of Enlightenment, or Buddhism.

In the view of the Mahāyāna tradition of Tibet, Buddhist ethics—the standard of moral conduct and philosophy of the Bodhisattva[2] path—has more meaning and applications than simply that of moral behavior. Mahāyāna philosophy classifies the whole universe into two truths, relative truth and absolute truth.

The relative truth is the conventional aspect of the universe as we mundane beings experience it in our day-to-day life. The absolute truth is the ultimate meaning of the universe, the true nature, the enlightened state or Buddhahood. It can be achieved as the result of a spiritual approach.

For people of the mundane world the ethical applications of Buddhism are means to improve our spiritual and social conduct and to lead us to enlightenment. In Buddhahood the ethical applications have been perfected spontaneously, and the Buddha's beneficial services appear to all beings who are open to them, without effort, and with the ethical character appropriate to each being.

The relative truth denotes phenomena appearing and functioning in interdependent causation. It is false and illusory, because for those who have realized the absolute truth, phenomena do not appear as we mundane beings view them.

The absolute truth is characterized as the true nature of the universe, the Buddha-essence, and emptiness (voidness). It is absolute nature, which is the realized state of enlightenment, and it transcends the mundane mind, the effects of causation, and the distinctions of time and space. Different schools have different ways of defining absolute truth. According to Prāsaṅgika, absolute truth is emptiness free from the elaborations of all mental distinctions. For Cittamātra, it is the thoroughly established Buddha-essence. In Mahāsandhi (*rDzogs-Pa Ch'en-Po*), it is the Buddha-essence free from conceptual elaborations. Although the interpretations are different, they signify the same Buddha-essence, which is emptiness, free from elaborations.

Are these two truths separate? For mundane beings they appear to be two different things: relative truth, which is known to us, and absolute truth, which is incomprehensible. But in their true meaning, for an enlightened person, they are as one, the union of two truths or the union of emptiness and appearances (*sNang sTong*). The whole universe is one in the great freedom of Buddhahood, the pure and true nature of the universe, which has no limits or discriminations. And the whole conventional universe appears and functions spontaneously and simultaneously whenever the causes are present, within the union of the two truths. The Buddha sees them all simultaneously without apprehension and conceptual grasping. For an enlightened one, appearances are the spontaneous appearances of emptiness or Buddha-essence. And the emptiness and openness is a spontaneous appearance without being contrived, as is the limited and discriminated world. It is like colorful lights appearing from a clear crystal ball if it is touched by sunlight. Of this the Buddha said:

> Emptiness is form and form is emptiness.

Mundane beings need to follow ethical norms in order to increase their spiritual strength, but all of the Buddha's conduct spontaneously appears as "perfection," and this is called the Buddha action. Similarly, we have to turn on a light to see things, but for the sun the light is there spontaneously.

The writings included in this book are mainly based on Buddhist ethical disciplines, but some are concerned with secular ethics and even local ethnic cultural values.

1. The Heart-Essence: Advice on Two Ethics

This text, *Zhal-gDams Lugs-gNyis sNying-bChud,* was written by Paltrul Rinpoche (dPal sPrul Rin-Po-Ch'e, 1808–1887), one of the greatest meditation masters and writers of the Nyingmapa school.

Paltrul Rinpoche's full name, given by the first Dodrup Chen Rinpoche, was Jigme Chokyi Wangpo ('Jigs-Med Ch'os-Kyi dBang-Po). He was born into one of the Dzachu Kha nomadic tribes and was recognized as the reincarnation of Palge of Dzogchen monastery by Dola Jigme Kalzang (alias Chokyi Lodrö). In the biography by his student, the third Dodrup Chen, he is described as follows:

> His head is broad like a parasol. His face is like a blossoming lotus and his sense faculties are very clear. Usually he has very little sickness. From childhood he has been endowed with great wisdom, compassion, and courage. He has great confidence and is a brilliant orator. (DN3a/3)

He studied the wisdom of all the Buddhist traditions of Tibet with great sages and scholars of eastern Tibet including: Jigme Kalzang, Jigme Ngotshar, Gyalse Zhenphen Thaye, and the fourth Dzogchen Rinpoche. In particular, he received the lineal transmissions of wisdom and realization from Jigme Gyalwe Nyuku and Do Khyentse Yeshey Dorje. He received the explanations of the preliminary practice of Longchen Nyingthig twenty-five times from Jigme Gyalwe Nyuku. He was introduced to the highest realization of "the clear, sky-like all-pervading intrinsic awareness" by Do Khyentse.

Then he renounced his obligations at the monastery and became a hermit. He wandered all over Golok and tamed the violent Golok tribespeople with the Dharma[3] and caused the Dharma to flourish. For three years he presided over and taught at the forty-five-day seminary on *Guhyagarbha-tantra* practice at Yarlung Pema Kö, the original Dodrup Chen's monastery. The seminary was established by Gyalse Zhenphen Thaye, and Paltrul Rinpoche was his teaching assistant. He also spent some time at Shugchen Tago monastery and Ari Nag hermitage in the Do valley.

He went not only to the scholars and established Dharma institutions but also to people who didn't even have the opportunity to learn simple prayers, and he taught them how to say OṂ MAṆI PADME HŪṂ.

Then he went back to Dzogchen monastery and taught scriptures at the famous Śrīsiṇha college, Pame Thang, Nagchung hermitage, and other institutions of the Dzogchen monastery.

Finally, he spent most of the later part of his life in Dzachu Kha, the beautiful and vast nomadic grassland of his native tribal community. He spent years sponsoring and supervising the construction of a huge hundred-thousand–OṂ MAṆI PADME HŪṂ stone wall (*Mani'i rDo-'Bum*). He stayed at and taught at Gegong hermitage, Dzagya monastery, Changma Lung hermitage, Komo'i Oli, and other places in the Dzachu Kha valley. On the eighteenth day of the fourth month of the Fire Pig year (1887) he passed into the great peace, the ultimate nature.

Paltrul Rinpoche wrote six volumes of treatises on various subjects: philosophy, poetry, ethics, and esoteric teachings (tantras). In eastern Tibet he was perhaps the most instrumental of anyone in making the *Bodhicaryāvatāra* ("The Ways of Bodhisattva Training") a handbook for many monks, "The Aspirational Prayer for Taking Rebirth in the Blissful Pure Land" a daily prayer for many lay people, the *Guhyagarbha-tantra* the foundation of Nyingmapa tradition, Dzogpa Chenpo teachings not only a textual tradition but a live practice, and, above all, OṂ MAṆI PADME HŪṂ the perpetual breathing of all.

The third Dodrup Chen Rinpoche records that although

Paltrul Rinpoche was the most humble person, to his close disciples he admitted to possessing many enlightened powers: that he no longer had any emotional defilements, remembered over a hundred previous lives, and knew where deceased persons have taken rebirth. The third Dodrup Chen describes Paltrul's lectures:

> Whatever lectures he delivers, he never presents them with any trace of showing off his scholarship but with a view to how they suit the listeners' understanding. If his lectures are checked by a scholar, they are meaningful. If they are heard by a dull mind, they are easy to understand. As they are condensed, they are easy to catch. They are of adequate length, related to the subject, enchanting, and tasteful. (DN13b/3)

The third Dodrup Chen also describes Paltrul's personality:

> He uses fearful and overwhelmingly tough words, but there is no trace of hatred or attachment in them; and if one knows how to listen to them, they are only direct and indirect instructions. Whatever he says is solid like gold—it is true, he treats all people equally, neither flattering them in their presence nor backbiting in their absence, and he never pretends to be something or someone else. So everybody, high or low, respects him as an authentic master. He is not partial to the faces and minds of high people nor does he have contempt for ordinary people. Whoever is involved in unvirtuous activities, unless the person is unchangeable, he digs out his faults at once. He praises and inspires people who are pursuing a spiritual life. He seems hard to serve, yet however close you are to him, it is impossible to find a single instance of partiality, doubt, change, or contradiction in him. He is unchanging in friendship, easy to be with, relaxing, and has patience concerning both good and bad occurrences. It is hard to separate from him. . . . In brief, although he remained a hidden practitioner all his life, he was as a proverb says: "Even if gold remains underground, its light radiates into the sky." Because he never deviated from his Bodhisattva activities, he was wholesome from every point of view. To

> the extent that you examine him, you will find him clean and pure. To the extent that you think about him, your faith in him increases. (DN15a/5)

Among his chief disciples were: Wonpo Tendzin Norbu (Tenga), Khenpo Pema Damcho Özer, Mipham Rinpoche (1846–1912), Nyoshul Lungtog, the third Dodrup Chen (1865–1926), the fifth Dzogchen Rinpoche (1872–?), Adzom Drugpa (1842–?), Khenpo Zhenphen Chokyi Nangwa (Zhen-ga) (1871–1927), Thubten Chokyi Tragpa, and Alag Do-ngag Gyatsho.

The *Heart-Essence* is ethical advice for people of all ages but especially for young people. The author has written this text in the form of a dialogue between a youth filled with pride and contemptuous of others and an experienced, gentle, and wise old man. The wise old man shocks the boy by telling him that when he himself was young, he was more handsome and bright than the boy.

> When I had the flesh and blood of youth,
> I was more handsome than you.
> When my tongue, eyes, and senses were clear,
> I was brighter than you.

Then he lets the boy calm down and leads his wild mind into the beauty of ethics. Although the title of this text is *The Heart-Essence: Advice on Two Ethics* (i.e., the Buddhist and the secular ethics), the text states clearly that it is advice only on worldly ethics (i.e., nonreligious, social, and secular ethics). It says:

> As for spiritual [Dharma] ethics, there are endless canonical scriptures . . . , so it is not necessary for me to muddle along trying to talk about them. So now I shall tell you about worldly ethics in brief.

However, because of the ethical background of the author himself and the culture of Tibet, all the advice is based on or influenced by Buddhist terms and values. Furthermore, there are some lines that express purely Buddhist principles:

> The human body, difficult to obtain, is only for this
> one time;
> Keep the precepts of *upavasatha* and *upāsaka*.

Nevertheless, this text could be classified mainly as secular ethical advice seen through the eyes of Buddhist wisdom. The author uses many popular and delightful folk proverbs of local tribal people of eastern Tibet and also quotations from Buddhist sayings to illustrate and support his views.

For this translation I have used an edition that was transcribed by Chatral Changchub Dorjey, a learned lama from Golok who now lives in Bhutan. He wrote the text from memory, as no written copies survived, and then asked Kyabje Dudjom Rinpoche (1904–1987) to edit it. In 1984, when I saw Kyabje Rinpoche for the last time in New York, he went through the text again and made some more corrections, which I have followed.

2. Holy Dharma Advice: A Drama in the Lotus Garden

This text, *Lha-Ch'os Dang mThun-Pa'i gTam Padma'i Tshal-Gyi Zlos-Gar Zhes-Bya-Ba,* was also written by Paltrul Rinpoche. In it he presents the tragic story of two honeybees: a golden bee, Wide Wings, the male, and a turquoise bee, Sweet Lotus Voice, the female. He gives a vivid image of the sincere, innocent, carefree, fragile, and tragic lives of two bees. They receive spiritual inspiration from the teachings of a learned sage, Dönkun Trubpa (Don-Kun Grub-Pa), but their days are passed in playing around gardens, enjoying the honey of the flowers in each other's company. One day, all of a sudden, the life of Lotus Voice ends in a tragic death, leaving Wide Wings alone in grief, experiencing the nature of saṃsāra,[4] the sorrow of the world. This incident awakens in the heart of the lonely honeybee the understanding that the value of an emotional and egoistic samsaric life is an unreliable one of change and suffering, and that the true goal or essence of life lies in the positive energies of the spiritual attainments of the Dharmic path and in the results of Buddha attainments.

The bees knew their life was going to end but never expected it to happen so suddenly. They knew that samsaric life is full of suffering, but they didn't expect it would be so cruel to them.

They knew and believed in spiritual values, and those values were what they wished to pursue, but the pleasure of the world was too attractive to them to resist. When their dream life breaks into pieces it is too late to do anything but lament. At last Wide Wing's mind turns to the path of enlightenment, but it takes the death of his beloved wife to cause the turning.

This text also demonstrates how close Buddhism is to the life of nonhuman beings such as bees, and how deeply Buddhists feel the experience of an animal or an insect, as of a human heart.

The original text is written in Tibetan in very beautiful poetic language, but its beauty fades away in translation.

The metaphorical figures, places, and events in this text represent the lives of real people.[5] Trashi Deleg, a young man who was the son of a rich and powerful family called Zimpon Tshang from the Dan valley ('Dan Khog) in Dege province, married the beautiful twenty-five-year-old daughter of Gonpo Dargye of the Jutshang family. Soon after, many people of the valley perished in an epidemic and the young bride was one of the casualties. Aggrieved, Trashi Deleg went to Paltrul Rinpoche, who was in retreat in Pema Shelphug (Crystal Lotus Cave) at Pema Ri (Lotus Peak), a sacred mountain in the Dan valley. From Paltrul Rinpoche he received teachings and devoted the rest of his life to Dharma practice. At the request of Trashi Deleg, Paltrul Rinpoche wrote this text based on the experiences of Trashi Deleg and his bride as a teaching for future disciples.

The real identities of some of the subjects metaphorically portrayed in this text are as follows: Paltrul Rinpoche is Lotus Joy, Dzachukha valley is the Flower Garden of the Northern Plain, and the Dan valley is the Pleasure Garden of Lotus Heap. Some of the families of the tribal group of this area are represented by various kinds of lotuses. Trashi Deleg is represented by Wide Wings, his bride by Sweet Lotus Voice, Dzagya (rDza rGya) monastery in Dzachu Kha valley by a hermitage known as Medicinal Eye Drops, the epidemic by a shadow of dark clouds followed by a gale, a lama from Ragdo (Rag-mDo) by a raven, the monks of Chokhor Ling (Ch'os 'Khor Gling) monastery in Dan valley by a flock of sparrows, a Chö[6] practitioner from Palyul Ragchab (dPal-Yul Rag-Ch'ab) by a frog, a doctor called Tshepag by a serpent, a lama retreatant called Chödar by a marmot, a diviner called Trashi by a cuckoo, a doctor called Phende Gyatsho by a wild horse, a performer of Dö (mDos) ritual called Sangye Kyab by a black spider, and a Chö practitioner from Dan Shug-ra ('Dan Shug-Ra) by a kite. According to H. H. Dilgo Khyentse Rinpoche, the sage known as the All Knowing One refers to a great adept called Lama Akar from Dzachu Kha Valley.

This text presents a very significant method of spiritual psychotherapy from the wisdom of a great Buddhist mind from the isolated nomadic land of Tibet. Paltrul takes the reader through feelings of missed opportunities, failures, and the pains of life. He lets the reader touch and feel the thread of an individual life, in this case a sorrowful one because of the loss of a loved one. Then he lets the reader get out of the feeling of locked-in pain by showing him the character of saṃsāra as an unreliable, suffering, and changing nature. This evokes the feeling that it is not something unexpected or an individual tragedy that has happened but the natural course of things that will befall us all. Then he lets the reader see the positive aspects of the negative happenings so as to transform their effects into a source of positive energy:

> Happiness is not good, suffering is good.
> If you are happy, the five poisonous emotions rage.
> If you suffer, previously accumulated evil deeds are
>   exhausted. . . .
> Praise is not good, blame is good.
> If praised, then pride and arrogance increase.
> If blamed, then one's own faults are exposed.

Finally, introducing the reader into the path of Buddhism, which leads through the path of joy to the result of joy, the author writes:

> For the deity, keep the powerful Buddha of
>   Compassion.

For the prayers, recite the six syllables.
For the training, meditate on loving-kindness and compassion.
Then even if you desire suffering, you will experience happiness.

3. Beautiful Garland of Flowers: Advice on Two Ethics

This short text of advice, *Lugs-gNyis Kyi bSlab-Bya Me-Tog 'Phreng-mDzes Zhes-Bya-Ba,* was written by Jigme Thrinle Özer ('Jigs-Med Phrin-Las A'od-Zer), the first Dodrup Chen Rinpoche (1745–1821), who was one of the greatest of the accomplished masters, the principal doctrine holder of the Longchen Nyingthig cycle of teachings and a Dharma Treasure Discoverer (*gTer-sTon*). He was also known as Dola Kunzang Zhenphen (rDo-Bla Kun-bZang gZhan-Phan), Changchub Dorje (Byang-Ch'ub rDo-rJe), and Drubwang Dzogchenpa (Grub-dBang, rDzogs-Ch'en-Pa).

He was born in the Do valley, into a chieftain family of the Buchung clan, famous as a warrior lineage of Golok province in eastern Tibet. The third Dodrup Chen summarizes the childhood of the first Dodrup Chen Rinpoche:

At his birth he remembered his previous lives.
He was greatly compassionate. By merely studying the alphabet
He perfected his reading skills. (FWT 6a/5)

At twenty-one he went to Dag-Iha Gampo, the monastery built by Gampopa (1079–1153), and received teachings. Then from a number of teachers, including the third Dzogchen Rinpoche, he received many teachings and transmissions, and practiced them at different caves and hermitages. Highly inspired by *Yönten Dzö,* he went to central Tibet to meet the author, Rigdzin Jigme Lingpa. Jigme Lingpa recognized Dodrup Chen as the reincarnation of Prince Murum Tsenpo, one of the three sons of King Thrisong Deutsen, and transmitted and entrusted the Longchen Nyingthig cycle of teachings to him as the principal doctrine holder. When Dodrup Chen performed ritual ceremonies, signs were witnessed that pacified the Nepalese war against Tibet and ended the drought in central Tibet. From then on he was known as Dodrup Chen (rDo Grub-Ch'en), the Great Saint from Do Valley. He is responsible for spreading the Nyingma tantras and especially the Longchen Nyingthig teachings in Kham, Golok, Amdo, and Gyarong and among some Mongolian tribal groups.

The first Dodrup Chen discovered a cycle of teachings that are Mind Dharma Treasures known as *Damchö Dechen Lamchog* (*Dam-Ch'os bDe-Ch'en Lam-mCh'og*). In addition he wrote a commentary on *Yönten Dzö.* He built several monasteries and spent his last many years at Yarlung Pema Kod monastery in the Ser valley. The monastery built by the second Dodrup Chen Rinpoche became known as Dodrup Chen monastery, a famous institution of learning in Golok province.

Among the first Dodrup Chen's great number of famous disciples were Do Khyentse Yeshey Dorje, Dola Jigme Kalzang (Chokyi Lodrö), Gyalse Zhenphen Thaye (1800–?), the fourth Dzogchen Rinpoche, Choying Tobden Dorje, Darma Seng-ge, the Mongol king Ngagwang Dargye (d. 1807), and Alag Shar Ngawang Tendar Lharampa (1759–?).

As stated in its Tibetan title, *Beautiful Garland of Flowers* is about both secular and spiritual moral disciplines. Many lines refer equally to secular and spiritual moral views, and some are exclusively about Buddhist ethics. But the unusual character of the text, written by such a prominent Buddhist master of Tibet, is that most of the advice given in it is secular or non-Buddhist; furthermore, some of it is based on local culture.

A point based on Buddhist belief:

> If you hold the Triple Gem[7] as your refuge, all your wishes will be achieved.

The same point, based on mutual values:

> If you refrain from jealousy, your mind will be at ease.

And based on a secular view:

> Do not challenge those enemies who are unconquerable.

And based on local culture:

> Do not disturb the lord of nature and the land, as it may cause lightning and hailstorms.

This text demonstrates that a great master can objectively provide the most needed and soothing advice without being subjective and rigid in his Buddhist way of valuation.

4. Reminder to Son Śrī

This short text of advice on Buddhist ethics (*Bu Śrī Yid-La Nges-rGyu*) was also written by Paltrul Rinpoche. Except for a few lines on Buddhism at the beginning, the text consists mostly of moral teachings that apply equally to Dharma and social values. The author has arranged three pieces of advice under each category. For example:

> There are three things that should be in conformity: Your talks with friends, clothes with the country, and mind with Dharma.

5. Instructional Advice on Training in Buddhism

This short text of advice for practitioners of Buddhist training was also written by Paltrul Rinpoche. The title of this text is added by the translator because the original is untitled. Principally it shows which teachings of Buddhism are essential to practice and exhorts you to practice what you have been taught until it reaches fruition.

Some of the advice given in this text seems prophetically intended for today's Western Buddhist friends. It exhorts you to urge yourself to practice the teachings you have received until you have an experiential result, and not to run out hunting for more teachings until you have got the real taste of the teaching you have already received.

6. A Letter of Spiritual Advice

This letter of spiritual advice was written by Lobzang Thubten Lungtog Gyatsho, popularly known as Lauthang Tulku Rinpoche, as he was from Lauthang monastery, near Dartsedo (Chinese: Tachinlu) in eastern Tibet. He wrote this letter to me, Tulku Thondup, in 1954.

Lauthang Tulku is one of the incarnations of the second Dodrup Chen Rinpoche. He studied with many scholars at many monasteries in both eastern and central Tibet, but his main teacher was Khenpo Kome (1859–1936) of Dodrup Chen monastery. He became a great scholar but lived as a hermit in a hermitage near Lauthang monastery.

I never met Lauthang Tulku Rinpoche, but we used to communicate by writing. As reflected in this letter, as a traditional Tibetan Buddhist master he was respectful and kind to me because I was recognized as the reincarnation of Kome Khenpo, his principal teacher. The message he conveys in this letter is a description of his teacher's tradition, and advice to me to follow it. So it is appropriate to say a few words about Kome Khenpo.

Khenpo Kome is also known as Lushul Khenpo, Lobzang Kunkhyab, and Konchog Dron-me (Kome). Because his parents migrated from the Do valley to Dzachu Kha, he was born in the Lushul tribal group of Dzachu Kha. But later his family returned to the Do valley, where he became a monk at Dodrup Chen monastery. He studied with Paltrul Rinpoche, Khyentse'i Wangpo (1820–1892), Gyawa Alag Do-ngag Gyatsho, and the third Dodrup Chen. He became a great scholar and taught during his whole life. He wrote many scholarly texts, but only one commentary on the Yumka sādhana has survived. Almost all the scholars and Khenpos of the 1930s and 1940s in the Golok area were the protégés of Kome Khenpo. He used to meditate until noon and then would teach, sometimes seven classes, till dusk. He is well known for being a greatly accomplished meditator. Through the practice of Cakrasaṃvara, he accomplished the state of illusory-body (*rGyu-Lus*), which enabled him to travel to various Buddha lands by transferring his consciousness into the divine body of the deity. He had divine eyes, which enabled him to see the beings of various realms. He was a highly accomplished Dzogpa Chenpo meditator, and as a result he left signs, such as relics (*Ring-bSrel* and *gDungs*) in four different colors, at the time of his death.

A Letter of Spiritual Advice is written in very beautiful Tibetan poetry with advice on leading a proper spiritual life of learning and training. It is spiritual advice presented, as an offering to the addressee, with high veneration. It shows how a nonsectarian master and monastery can study and practice the teachings of different schools of Tibetan Buddhism as parts of one nectar, the same teaching. In the spiritual world, there are many individuals or institutions that claim to be proponents of nonsectarianism, while in practice they exclude others' spiritual traditions. Often when nonsectarianism is made an issue, the feeling of sectarianism creeps in. At Dodrup Chen monastery the issue of sectarianism or nonsectarianism was nonexistent. All the teachings were accepted as though they were different parts of the same candy. In this letter, the author urges me to maintain the teaching tradition of Khenpo Kome. He shows that at Dodrup Chen monastery, an important Nyingmapa monastery, Khenpo Kome maintained a curriculum that started from sutric teachings, such as "The Stages of the Path" by Tsongkhapa, founder of the Gelugpa school, and ended with the teachings on Dzogpa Chenpo, the "Great Perfection" of the Nyingma school.

7. Instructions on Turning Happiness and Suffering into the Path of Enlightenment

This text, *sKyid-sDug Lam-Khyer Gyi Man-Ngag,* was written in Tibetan by Jigme Tenpe Nyingma (1865–1926), the third Dodrup Chen Rinpoche, a renowned Buddhist scholar and writer of the Nyingmapa school.

He was one of the eight sons of Dudjom Lingpa (1835–1903), a great Dharma Treasure Discoverer (*gTer-sTon*) in Golok province of eastern Tibet. He studied with Paltrul Rinpoche, Khyentse'i Wangpo, the fourth Dzogchen Rinpoche, Do-ngag Gyatsho, Khenpo Pema Dorje, Mipham Rinpoche, and other scholars.

At the age of eight, he gave lectures on the *Bodhicaryāvatāra* to huge assemblies headed by his teacher Paltrul Rinpoche, and the fame of his wisdom started to reach all directions. At the age of twenty-one he wrote a famous commentary on the *Guhyagarbhamāyājāla-tantra*. Then, because of ill health, for the entire later part of his life he lived in seclusion at a hermitage near Dodrup Chen monastery called Gephel Rithrod, which in poetic writings he calls "The Forest of Many Birds"; there he gave audience to only a few great masters. He wrote many scholarly treatises and articles in five volumes. The most famous of his writings are "Elucidation of Memory" and "Outline of the *Guhyagarbhamāyājāla-tantra*." Among his disciples were the four great Khenpos of Dodrup Chen monastery, Gekong Khenpo Kunpal, and Khyentse Chokyi Lodrö (1893–1959).

The present text is a short but important and unique handbook of spiritual psychotherapy according to Buddhist teachings. Basing himself on the *Bodhicaryāvatāra* by Śāntideva, the *Ratnāvalī* by Nāgārjuna, and other important Mahāyāna teachings of Buddhism, the author presents various mental and spiritual approaches to dealing with one's negative perceptions, sensitive nature, and emotional experiences in order to turn them into tolerant, relaxed, positive, and perfect views and applications.

The text contains some Buddhist practices such as "Using Suffering as the Support of Going for Refuge" and "Contemplating the Absolute Truth," but most of the views and techniques discussed, such as "Avoiding Considering Suffering as Something Unfavorable," are applicable by people of any faith. Even those exercises that specifically incorporate Buddhist trainings such as "Going for Refuge" can also be applied by non-Buddhists, by relating them to their own object of faith, the source of positive views and strength.

In these troubled days, not only ordinary people but even many people in religious robes (sometimes they are even worse in lacking tolerance) experience happiness and sorrow in an ordinary way, full of hopes and excitements, fears and torments; they do not know how to make these situations work for their lives and for survival. Many people rush to get as much happiness as they can from "the honey at the razor's edge," such as worldly pleasures, and have no idea of the true aim of life. They fritter away their days in endless egocentric goals, become slaves to the toys of their extravagant world, and end up like a moth caught by the beauty of the candle flame. On the other hand, many people are oppressed by intolerable suffering, and sometimes find no escape other than by taking their own lives.

According to this text, to see and take suffering as the means of spiritual training is relatively easy. Experiences of suffering bring forth and enforce an awareness of the true character of the world, generate revulsion toward samsaric phenomena, and cause one to turn instead to spiritual trainings. The author also deals with the more difficult matter of seeing and applying the experiences of happiness as a means of spiritual training. It is harder to break away from happiness when one is glued to so-called pleasures by attachment, even though samsaric pleasures can be neither pure nor enduring. So in fact both happiness and suffering are deceptive and are obstacles to true or spiritual training and attainments.

If we can perfect the skill of our training in turning both happiness and suffering into the path of enlightenment, then, no matter what we face or experience in our relations with the outer world, our minds will remain calm, enlightened, and at ease, unperturbed either in happiness or in sorrow, as gold will shine wherever it is. To the unfortunate people of this dark age in which chaos and difficulties prevail, the trainings given in this text are most useful, bringing relief from the exhaustion of doubt and expectation, and guiding the mind to find rest in its natural state of purity and peace.

8. Entering into the Path of Enlightenment: Taking Daily Activities as the Path, According to the Unified Approach of Sūtra and Tantra

This text, *mDo-sNgags Zung-Du 'Jug-Pa'i sPyod-Yul Lam-Khyer Sangs-rGyas Lam-Zhugs Zhes-Bya-Ba,* on applying Buddhist training to everyday life, was written by Rigdzin Jigme Lingpa

(1729–1798), the Discoverer of the Dharma Treasures (*gTer-sTon*) of the Longchen Nyingthig teachings. He is one of the greatest teachers and writers of the Nyingma school.

He was born in southern Tibet amid many miraculous signs, such as being able to recollect his previous lives. At the age of ten he entered Palri monastery and studied secular subjects and Buddhist scriptures. At the age of twenty-eight Rigdzin Jigme Lingpa started a three-year retreat at Palri. He had many visions and gave signs of various accomplishments.

All phenomena turned into illusory existents as the illusory appearances of Buddha manifestations and the symbols of teachings. His speech burst forth words of profound meaning. At the age of twenty-eight, he discovered the Dharma Treasure Teachings (*gTer Ch'os*) of the Longchen Nyingthig cycle.

At the age of thirty-one he entered into another three-year retreat, in Sangchen Metog cave at Chimphu, near Samye monastery. During this retreat he received the body, speech, and mind, the total blessings, of Kunkhyen Longchen Rabjam in three successive pure visions, and became inseparable from the master. In this cave, for the first time, he gave the empowerments and teachings of the Longchen Nyingthig cycle to his disciples.

Considering the vastness and depth of his scholarship after comparatively little study of scriptures, he is regarded as an instant or naturally gifted (Rang-Byung) scholar. He holds the long transmissions of tantras passed down from masters to their disciples, and he also became a holder of short transmissions as he received the transmission of Nyingthig teachings in pure visions.

At the age of thirty-four he built a small hermitage-like monastery called Tshering Jong in southern Tibet, and there he spent most of the later part of his life.

There are two or three huge volumes of Longchen Nyingthig teachings that he discovered as a Mind Dharma Treasure (*dGongs-gTer*). He wrote seven volumes of scholarly works, including the famous *Yönten Rinpoche'i Dzö* (*Yon-Tan Rin-Po-Ch'e'i mDzod*) with a two-volume autocommentary.

Among his great disciples were: the first Dodrup Chen

Rinpoche, Jigme Gyalwe Nyuku and Jigme Ngotshar from eastern Tibet, Kong-nyon Bepe Naljor from Kongpo, and Jigme Kuntrol from Bhutan.

His monastery was later turned into a nunnery. The Longchen Nyingthig became one of the best-known teaching traditions of the Nyingma school.

In this text, *Entering into the Path of Enlightenment,* the author gives instructions on how to think and act throughout the day, during off-meditative periods, starting from waking up in the morning until sleeping and dreaming at night, and from cooking a meal to going to the toilet. These instructions are based on the esoteric (tantric) training of Buddhism, which stresses mental attitudes and perceptions. It is not easy or even appropriate to practice this path unless one has been initiated into esoteric trainings and has instructions on them.

Some people might have problems with aspects of this text, such as dedicating one's defecations to spirits. But before imposing judgments through an inherited, rigid cultural philosophy, take a moment to look at the view and purpose that lies behind this process. It is not just giving away the impurities that one possesses, but is a part of the dedication of one's total life. In Buddhism the mind is the main factor and forerunner of all activities, so the aim is to apply oneself to the universal value of a mind of compassion, peace, openness, balance, and wisdom, without being trapped by cultural, racial, regional, emotional, or conceptual boundaries or walls. Also, it is believed and seen that many classes of beings, like spirits and insects, live on and use such things as their object of enjoyment, as bees are attracted to flowers and flies to filth. If we could use common sense free from prejudice, we would see that the views and methods of Buddhist training are universal and practical.

If we could follow the instructions of this text, every activity of life would be transformed and dedicated to the proper attitudes: compassion, caring, peacefulness, and having pure perception. Then there is no room for negative emotions and experiences: anger, jealousy, sadness, and so forth. If you are filled with positive and perfect energies and wisdom, then you will be a powerful and beneficial tool for serving all others.

In this text, the mantra(s) and dhāraṇī(s) are given with the proper Sanskrit spelling. For the Sanskrit mantra(s) and dhāraṇī(s) for recitation, their Tibetanized Sanskrit pronunciation has been provided in square brackets after the Sanskrit lines unless indicated otherwise.

1

The Heart-Essence
Advice on Two Ethics

Paltrul Rinpoche

In the famous Thramo Lingkar Tod [*Khra-Mo Gling-dKar sTod*] in the province of Dome [*mDo-sMad;* in eastern Tibet] there lived a family with a son named Zhönnu Loden [gZon-Nu Blo-lDan]. He was bright, good natured, and had all the skills of a gentle person. But because his parents died when he was young, he had no one to give him good advice; so he fell in with bad companions. He became involved in crude behavior such as stealing, lying, and cheating. One day while he was walking along a road, he met an old man with a white beard and white hair, holding a walking stick and moving along with doddering steps. Looking at the old man, the boy laughed and said:

> Ha! Ha! There's no winter frost,
> So you don't have to put on a lambskin hat!
> There's no fierce dog,
> So you don't have to carry a willow stick.
> There's no place to dance here,
> So you don't have to take tottering steps!
> Old man, which place do you belong to?
> Where are you coming from this morning?
> Where are you going tonight?
> Give me a straight answer and don't hide anything.

Then the old man stared with wide open eyes at the boy and said:

Ha! Ha! From the way you strut scornfully,
You seem to be young and proud.
Your witty style of joking and boasting
Makes you out to be clever but ill mannered.
From your sarcasm toward an old man,
It seems you have no parents, only bad friends.
Old age comes even to solid rocks.
Even the glossy fur of the youthful tiger fades.
There are good and bad sons of the same father.
When I had the flesh and blood of youth,
I was handsomer than you.
When my tongue, eyes, and senses were clear,
I was brighter than you.
When I had my own home and country,
I was more distinguished than you.
I am from Do Kham province.
This morning I have come from the City of Saṃsāra.
Tonight I am going to the Island of Liberation.

The young boy thought, "To hear him talk this way, he seems like a learned old man." He said to him, "Hey, old man, sit here awhile and tell me something."

The old man replied, "What shall I say? I don't know how to speak about Dharma. You won't listen to worldly advice. Better for an old man to go on his way."

The young boy promised, saying, "I really will listen to whatever you say."

Then the old man slowly sat down and said, "Oh, I don't have the knowledge to say much about the Dharma or the world—even though I know that all the people of this dull age are following a way of crude and evil conduct, and are just passing their time with selfish and cunning thoughts; that they harbor only thoughts of ill will and are acting in perverted ways. This is the age of popularity of the bad rather than the good, the age of victory for shameless rather than honest people, the age of preferring new friends over those to whom we owe gratitude. Now the rule of the higher authorities is chaotic and the behavior of the subjects is disordered. Forgetting about the next life, people praise as heroic the activities of men who are shameless and stupid. And if someone seeks advice about good conduct, not only do people think it foolish, but many are not even aware that there are worldly ethics to be learned. In this evil age, it is useless for a man like me to speak. But as a proverb has it:

> There is no choice but to do much talking when
> questioned by a friend.
> Foxes have no choice but to yelp when demons slap
> their cheeks!
> Dogs can't help barking when they see a dark shadow.

So, since you ask me, I should tell you. The saying goes:

> If asked, one should tell;
> If a man studies, he should be taught.

"Now, to tell you briefly about spiritual ethics: First, the teacher of spiritual ethics is the virtuous friend, the lama. And the source is the Buddha's doctrine. Second, one should practice repentance, develop Bodhi mind,[1] pure view, meditation, and so on, which are the roots of the Pratimokṣa, Bodhisattva, and tantric disciplines, appropriate to the lesser, medium, and high intelligence of individual minds. Finally, the elimination of the roots of defilement of one's own mind is the attainment of enlightenment. This is the condensation of the methods of all holy doctrines.

"About worldly ethics: First, the teachers of worldly ethics are the parents and the older generation. And the source is the ethical writings of the holy kings, ministers, and Bodhisattvas of ancient times. Second, all kings, ministers, and subjects, the higher and the lower, the rich and the poor, in proportion to their degree, should act according to the ethic of respecting the higher and serving the lower, and of associating with equals. Finally, to set out on the path that leads to happiness in this life and to Liberation in the next is the condensation of worldly ethics.

"As for spiritual ethics, there are endless canonical scriptures and commentaries, texts, and instructions; so it is not necessary for me to muddle along trying to talk about them. So now I shall tell you about worldly ethics in brief."

Worldly Ethics

The Ethic of Respect for Superiors

"For those who are higher or lower, good or bad, there is no source of hope or object of support in this life or the next other than the Three Jewels. Therefore, one should pay respect and homage, and make offerings with one-pointed faith to the objects of the Body, Speech, and Mind [of the Buddhas, Bodhisattvas, and Sages], such as images, holy scriptures, and stupas, whether they are old or new or of good or bad quality. For, as it is said [in the *Bodhicaryāvatāra*]:

> Whoever develops devotion,
> The Sage [Buddha] will be present before him.

"It is especially improper to be faithless, critical, or contemptuous of the good and bad qualities of lamas, monks, and religious persons. For they are the custodians of the consciousness of the dead, the objects of requests for protection by the living, the objects of offering for those who have, and the objects of supplication for those who have not. In this world there is no more sacred object than the Three Jewels. If one performs a small act of faith and devotion to them or accumulates merit, or if one speaks critically or with ill will of the Three Jewels, the results will be unimaginable. Their good and bad qualities cannot be distinguished by men like us. The gracious Buddha said:

> Except by me or one like me, it is not proper for men to be judged by men.

"Even when one perceives some seeming impurity, one should develop pure perception and devotion. Do not allow yourself to degenerate, and the faults of others will not harm you. There is no more serious fault either in spiritual or in worldly ethics than trying to find the faults of others and defaming them.

> It is not the faults of others, but one's own faults—
> Like reflections rising in the surface of a mirror.

"If you tell someone the faults of another, and if he is a thoughtful person, he may appear to agree with you, but actually he will be disgusted. For he may think by the way you're talking that you are two-faced. So it is said:

> Do not think of other's faults but of your own;
> Do not dig up anyone's misdeeds but your own.

"In your behavior toward all the chieftains, kings, ministers, leaders, the older generations of the country, parents, teachers, and spiritual friends, you should show respect, open the doors for them, arrange their seats, welcome them, see them off, show them faith and respect, and conduct yourself humbly and circumspectly. Nowadays, some people, considering themselves high or scholarly or rich, show contempt for everybody else. Actually, in doing so their own faults are exposed, proving that they possess neither spiritual nor worldly virtues. For example, it is said:

> Those without virtues will have great pride;
> Empty husks will hold their heads high.

And:

> On the peak of pride the water of virtue will not stay.

"Tibet never had a man who had more power, riches, and goodness than Chogyal Thrisong Deutsan [790–858].[2] Yet he showed respect to and prostrated himself before a yogi who lived like a beggar. For others he enacted a law of Sixteen Principles of Pure Human Conduct. So you should look up to your superiors and provide good examples for the future. Thus, those who are cultivated will have a gentle nature, an honest disposition, and a broad mind."

THE ETHIC OF SERVICE TO ORDINARY PEOPLE

"You should not have contempt or hatred for or abuse those who are weaker, more helpless, poorer, or more beggarly than yourself. And you should try to provide them with all the benefits of either speech, food, or clothes. In the event that you cannot help them, you should be polite and honest. The use of force, threats, or violence against weaker people and pretending to be a brave man is self-destructive. So it is said:

> A bad knife is sharp to the hand,
> A bad dog is fierce to beggars,
> A bad man is wrathful to the weak.

And:

> If you wish to be high, take the lower place;
> If you want victory, you must accept defeat.

"Seeing the bit of wealth, position, and power of others, and covering one's mouth with astonishment; seeing the weak, beggars, and miserable people, and looking down on them with one's nose in the air; getting excited over little things—these are signs of not having any experience of high and low fortune or of the happiness and suffering of the world. Whatever you see, high or low, good or bad, you should not be too fond of the high nor too repelled by the low, because happiness and sorrow, good and bad, will happen to you. It is rare for high or low position, happiness or sorrow, riches or poverty to last for a whole lifetime. As it is said:

> It is rare to maintain harmony for a long time;
> It is rare for a rich man to be happy for his whole life;
> It is rare for a scholar never to make a mistake.

THE ETHIC OF ASSOCIATION WITH EQUALS

"In relation to your relatives, friends, countrymen, and neighbors you should never steal, lie, cheat, create discord, be shameless or untrustworthy, backbite, deride, or abuse. You should try to do for all of them whatever you can that is beneficial. And you should not be quick to feel happiness or unhappiness over slight actions of theirs. You should be able to bear happiness and unhappiness and have room in yourself for good and bad eventualities. You should not get involved in doing everything that comes into your mind. Instead, be stable and single-minded. You should be harmonious with everyone, and not lose your modesty. It is important to examine situations by putting others in your position and yourself in the position of others. Whoever you are, you should recognize your own faults. People have a sharp pointer for showing others' faults, but it is very rare for them to have a mirror in which to see their own. If you do not examine yourself, there will be no one who will point them out to you. People may flatter you to your face, but behind your back there will be only backbiting and detraction. When people's faults are revealed to them straightforwardly with good intentions, rather than listen they will treat it as enmity. As it is said:

> A guilty man gets angry;
> A horse with sores on its back rears up.

"Nowadays people consider themselves perfect, but you should reform your mind by studying the ethical scriptures of scholars and watching your own nature. Do you understand?"

Then Zhönnu Loden said, "All right, that is the way to deal with higher, middling, and lower people. But nowadays many people, such as chieftains, will punish us severely with beatings and confiscation for a small misdemeanor, even if we have always been obedient and performed many services. Also, in the case of lower people like beggars and middling people like relatives and friends, even if we help them as much as we can, as though they were our own sons, many of them treat us like enemies by stealing our wealth, snatching our wives, and cheating us. So tell me, what should we do?"

Then the old man said, "O intelligent boy! It is good that you ask in such a thoughtful way. For it is difficult to understand just by listening. First you should consider the qualities of people, regardless of whether they are of high, middle, or low rank. Among them are the excellent, the mediocre, and the inferior. The excellent person will work for the country and the people, and his own interests will automatically be achieved. Without harming others, mediocre people will achieve their wishes. Inferior people will attempt to satisfy only their own interests by harming others, but still it will be difficult for them to achieve what they want. But in some cases vicious people will struggle persistently to achieve their own self-interest, suppressing all modesty or shame. They may partially accomplish their aim, but then they will be defamed by others. In each category there are three levels of quality. And also there are three classifications according to both spiritual and worldly ethics.

"Nowadays when someone is praised it raises him to the middle of the blue sky; and if someone is criticized it drives him down under the deep earth. People don't know how to assign things their rightful place. This is the fault of narrow-mindedness. It is said:

> Do not praise an unknown person too soon;
> Do not express happiness or unhappiness to a friend
> too soon.

"Even excellent lamas and chieftains will have some bad quality. Even among bad people like thieves and beggars there will be no one who does not have a good quality. But we have to find out who has more good qualities and who has more bad. It is said:

> A man who has good qualities but no bad ones is rare;
> A tree that has grown up straight with no gnarl is rare;
> Tempered iron, sharp and flexible, is rare!

"It is difficult to understand the mind of a scholar, the game of a cunning person, and the nature of a man who disguises it. So you should examine people by various methods, directly or indirectly.

> If you know how to examine whatever happens,
> this experience will make you happy;
> If you know how to examine whatever you learn,
> this familiarity will make you happy.

"If you don't examine things meticulously like that, it will be difficult to gain understanding.

If you don't encounter enemies and demons,
Anybody can be self-reliant.
If it is not a matter of property or labor,
Anybody can talk generously.
If you don't get caught in a lawsuit,
Anybody can be eloquent.
If you don't have to face a serious situation,
Anybody can be a good person in his mother's kitchen.

"One should carefully consider what is right or wrong without deciding hastily.

"Leaders, including officials of high rank, should be of few words, broad-minded, independent, well intentioned, and meticulous. Especially in matters of taxes and justice, they should not cherish their own interests or be influenced by wealth and rank, but be examples of honest conduct.

If there is no ruler, who will save the heads of the
  subjects?
If there are no subjects, whom shall the ruler govern?
If the ruler is honest, both ruler and subjects will be
  happy and strong.
If the subjects prosper, that is the ornament of
  kingship.
Good rulers will look after the welfare of their subjects.
Good subjects will act respectfully to the ruler.
If wood elevates wood, that is a pillar and beam;
If a man elevates another, that is a servant and master.

"The ruler and subjects should support one another like father and son. The older generation, fathers and uncles, should be sparing in speech and gentle. They should not leave problems like debts and lawsuits for their sons and grandsons. They should live comfortably and happily, practicing the pure Dharma in preparation for death. Men should be moderate in thought and action. They should be able to stand up to strong enemies. They should be patient in discussions with relatives and inferiors. They should have gentle natures and durable friendships. They should never lose their self-reliance.

If there is fighting among brothers, the shameless one will win.
Likewise, even if one is brave in defeating external enemies,
Only if he can accept defeat from his own relatives is he a good man.

"Women should be mentally calm and should not gossip a lot. They should regard their own husbands as divine and shun others' husbands as poison. They should be neat, good at saving, caring toward the servants and animals, humble, and modest.

"Subordinates, such as servants, should not have evil or cunning thoughts, lie or steal, backbite, or create enmity. A servant should be devoted to his master and listen to whatever he says, whether it is a large or small matter. Whatever his rank, high, middle, or low, a person should not be evil-minded, cunning, unstable, overly talkative, immoderate, or hot tempered.

It is pleasant if you have no angry friend;
It is comfortable if you have no lice-ridden clothes.

"In general what is good for one person will not be good for everybody, and what is bad for one person will not be bad for everybody. This is so because of the various results of the karma of individuals.

"Concerning enemies, some become enemies because of previous karma, others because of lack of understanding of their opponents, others because there was no alternative. Again, some become enemies because of discord created by others, or because of poor judgment. In the case of an enemy who is a cultivated person and is capable of friendship, you should calm his mind with friendly words and win him over as a friend by skillful means. Such is the behavior of learned people. If, however, the enemy is a bad or crude type of person, you should overcome him by gentle speech, a tough mind, and various clever methods. To subdue him forcefully by strength is the common way. Making promises without being able to keep them is foolish.

If you don't know how to speak, it's better to keep
quiet.
Work that you cannot accomplish is better not started.
Brave deeds that you cannot accomplish are better not
undertaken.

"As for relatives, you shouldn't praise them to their faces. And if they have faults you should point them out and try to correct their attitude. If they are worthy, try to help them with rewards and praise. In particular you should not spoil children and grandchildren, wife, and servants. And you should keep them in line with moderate treatment, neither too soft nor too strict. In the case of certain vicious people, it is actually better to discipline them strictly rather than gently.

When cymbals and drums are beaten, the sound is
sweet.
When walls and tent pegs are beaten they become
sturdy.
When leather and vicious people are beaten they
become tempered.
When children are properly disciplined, they become
obedient.

"In certain cases some foolish people do not appreciate a good family or friend, and will insult them and fight with them, causing the family or friend to become tired of them. But after they are separated they will feel regret. This is the sign of inability to establish a durable friendship.

If they associate too much, the lion will be insulted by
dogs;
If they are too close, the eye cannot see the eyebrow.

"There is nothing more important than to know the good and bad qualities of people. There are cases in which a single good person makes a community, village, or country happy; and there are cases in which a single bad person creates trouble among neighbors, community, and countries.

If you associate with excellent friends you will become excellent.
If you associate with evil friends you will become evil.
A virtuous friend is rarer than gold.
If he is on another side, make a friend of him.
An evil friend is worse than poison.
Even if he is on your side it is better to throw him away.

"So it is of primary importance to understand the good and bad qualities of your friends."

Then Zhönnu Loden said, "Please tell me how I should train myself in the action and conduct of moderation."

The old man said, "Oh ya! The action is coming, going, staying, working, subduing enemies, and serving relatives. The conduct is, for example, the manner of eating, drinking, sleeping, staying, speaking, and going. In both action and conduct you should examine what is good and bad yourself and ask others, take examples from the past, plan for the future, act according to your own ability, and abide by the system of the country. Do not fear powerful people or insult weak people. Determine the gain and loss, what can be done and what cannot; and if it is done, whether the result will be large or small. You should be careful from the beginning and try to say prayers for the success of an undertaking and the accumulation of merit.

In a speech the beginning is difficult;
In work the main part is difficult;
In Dharma the conclusion is difficult.

"So whatever task you have undertaken, until it is completed you should work with courage and patience. Your mind should not run after the many mouths of many people, and you should persevere for a long time with skill. In the end, if the work is good, then you should be satisfied. If you have failed, you should bear it without regret and without blaming others. There are only two ways for projects to succeed: by knowledge or by the strength of merit. The only means for one's own happiness in this life and the next is to accumulate merit through the Three Jewels.

> It is better to accumulate a spark of merit
> Than to make efforts the size of a mountain.

And:

> The purposes that are fulfilled by the strength of merit
> Will not depend on anything, like the light of the sun.
> The purposes that are fulfilled by the strength of efforts
> Will depend on many things, like the light of a butter lamp.

"People who are not wealthy should not be ambitious to eat fine food and put on fancy clothes. They should not indulge in crude and brainless activities like smoking, drinking, and gambling. You should earn and protect your own wealth day and night very strictly and carefully, and should not let it be lost uselessly or wasted. You should not lend to unreliable people, nor store with poor people things that are to be sold. If you seek wealth by theft or cunning, or because of jealousy, you will end up by losing not only wealth but your own life. If you have no previously accumulated good karma, you will not prosper merely by effort.

> Wealth cannot be acquired by mere accumulation, but by accumulation of merit.
> Clothes will not wear out by being put on, but because luck is exhausted.
> People do not die from illness, they die when the time comes.

"It is best for rich people to spend their wealth for holy Dharma as much as they can. The next best thing is to use it for the benefits of others. The least good is to use it for their own back and mouth. Otherwise, when one leaves all one's property to go naked and empty-handed to death, it is too late.

If your mind is covered by darkness,
Even a heap of wealth like Mount Meru will not help you.

"Generally, even if your mind is gentle, you should not lose your self-reliance. Do not be too hasty to express happiness or sorrow whenever good or bad arises. But you should distinguish between who does you good and who does you ill. It is wrong to repeat everything you have heard.

To say whatever comes into your mind is crazy.
To eat whatever you see is to be a dog or a pig.
To do whatever work you think of is brainless.

"Don't be too bold facing rivers, precipices, thieves, or wild beasts. Be careful even if the danger is small. Accept even minor assistance graciously. Do not say bad things about others in secret to anyone, good or bad. Be less talkative and more broad-minded. Except in special and important cases or when there is no choice, don't tell lies but speak honestly. Don't make many promises, but do whatever you have said so that it doesn't become a lie. Be brave for the sake of good people even if it costs you your wealth or labor. Reason with vicious people, and don't let them become obstinate. Receive strangers with respect and food, but don't lose property to them, and don't reveal your nature to them or tell your secrets. Do whatever you can to help people who are close to you, but don't make them disgusted with you or lie to them. When the position of others has diminished, do not abuse them. When you are flourishing and full-bellied, do not be selfish and proud. Don't try to challenge the solemn authority of lamas, chiefs, or tantric yogīs and Bönpos. Don't follow the man who is fickle and who is quick to feel happiness and sadness. Don't take everything that other people tell you as true. Don't consider whoever harms you as an enemy. Don't tell secrets even to people with whom you are on good terms. Even if you quarrel with someone, don't dig out his secret faults. Have no expectations of people who have gone away. Do not have short-lived loyalty to a person who has been helpful to you. Do not rely on a person whom you don't know well. Don't speak too much among many people. Don't be too busy when you are alone. Don't at any time undertake too many projects. Don't cheat the friends who believe in you. Don't hanker after the wealth of others. Whatever your work, do it in proportion to the job, and examine its purpose. Be sensitive to the feelings of your friends; you should be able to intuit other people's minds. Make use of your position. Even if you have no avarice, be very economical. You should be gentle but firm; honest and moderate.

"In general you should examine carefully the good and bad qualities of people. But nowadays most people do not inquire whether someone acts according to the ethics of a cultivated person. And if they receive a little help or benefit or are given a smile, they are quick to praise; but if their wishes are interfered with and something is done that they don't like, the abuse starts. Don't even listen to praise or disparagement that comes second-hand.

> Scholars know how to discriminate by themselves;
> Foolish people will follow what others say.
> When an old dog makes noise,
> For no reason other dogs will run.

And:

> If talk goes from mouth to mouth it will increase;
> If food goes from hand to hand it will decrease.

And:

> Any independence is a happy thing;
> All dependence on others involves sorrow.
> Common property is the root of quarrels.
> Promises are the cause of broken promises.
> The best wealth is contentment with what you have.
> The best quality is the spirit of benefiting others.
> The best ornament is knowledge.
> The best friend is the one without guile.
> The best happiness is developing the Bodhi mind.

And:

> Even among fools there will be wealthy ones;
> Among wild beasts some will be heroic.
> Animals, too, know how to satisfy their wishes.
> But the learned and gentle-mannered are rare in the world.

So please practice the ethic of gentle people."

Then Zhönnu Loden said, "Oh, I'm most thankful that you gave me these detailed instructions. But it is difficult to keep in mind so many instructions like these. So please tell them to me in a condensed form."

The old man said, "Oh, ya, you're right. Listen and I will tell you. Now, if worldly ethics are summarized, they can be included in five points:

1. A gentle nature
2. Moderation in action and conduct
3. A broad mind and stable nature
4. To be good at estimating work in advance
5. In all activities to have an honest and beneficial spirit

"1. If you are a man of angry and harsh words, you will not be in harmony with anyone. Even if you help people, they won't want to come near you. In the end no one will see you or keep you company. So it is necessary to have a gentle nature. A gentle nature means one whose nature is soft and relaxed, without angry or harsh words for anybody. But that doesn't mean that you should be like the leather of the musk deer, which goes in any direction that it is pulled; or like honey, which will stick to whatever touches it.

"2. To do a lot of work without moderation is risky. Sometimes the result will be profitable, but sometimes it will be a loss and nothing but an object of ridicule. So in friendships or activities you should act moderately and independently without many changes of mind. Moderation in work means that whatever work you do, you should know how to moderate it according to your own nature and ability and those of the other people involved. But it does not mean to be a bold, foolish man who will not be involved in any work.

"3. There is no one who does not desire food, wealth, women, and so forth. But in order to enjoy them you should consider the consequences and the need for being modest in behavior. There is no one who will not be angry at harsh words and harm done. But you should be concerned generally about the law and its punishments, and especially about the cause and result of karma in this life and the next. A stable person whose nature will not change in the midst of good or bad, happiness or sorrow, will certainly be praised by everyone in the end. So you should be stable without shifting in every direction. Stability means not running after whatever you think of or whatever anyone says, and that your activities and behavior are constant. It does not mean having a stick down your backbone so that you cannot bend.

"4. In all activities you should give consideration to the past and future. And you should examine all the gain and loss, good and bad, what will be beneficial and what will be harmful to yourself and to others now and in the future. If you know how to examine things you will achieve properly whatever you have in mind. Doing something without having time to examine it affects everyone, not only people like ourselves, but even kings. For example, King Pa-we Chin [dPa'-Ba'i Byin] and the King of Lańka saw the Bodhisattva Metog Dadzey [Me-Tog Zla-mDzes] and the Ṛiṣhi Zöpar Mawa [Drang-Srong bZod-Par sMra-Ba] in the company of their queens. They imagined that the Bodhisattva and the Ṛiṣhi wanted to keep the queens in their power through desire. The kings handed them over to executioners who killed them. Later the kings repented, but there was no way of atoning for their deed. There are also stories of people who listened to others and cheated with cunning. For example, the cunning Peme Tsalag [Padma'i rTsa-Lag] killed a woman named Zangmo [bZang-Mo] and threw the blood-stained knife in front of a sage named Gautama. And Gautama received the punishment. A thief stole a calf and left it in front of a

Pratyekabuddha who was living in a forest, then ran away. The Pratyekabuddha received the punishment. So, whatever work you do, you should be careful.

> Don't talk until you are certain that you understand.
> Don't take oaths until you are certain of their meaning.

"To examine means to know whether whatever work one starts will be completed or not; and if completed, what the outcome will be. If you shoot an arrow it should not fall on the ground. Whatever work you do should not collapse. But to examine does not mean to lack a mirror in which to see your own faults, while pointing out other people's faults and analyzing them cleverly.

"5. If you have an honest and altruistic mind, in whatever work you do for yourself or others, everybody's wishes will be achieved. In this life the Dharma Protectors will protect you and will make your name and fame flourish. Everyone will love and respect you, and you will automatically accomplish the Dharma for the next life. It is very important not to dissociate yourself from this good intention. If you have malice toward others, the consequences for yourself will be harsh. Beneficial thought means the good thought of giving help to all, high or low, good or bad, without considering whether they have helped you or are known to you. It is not just having love and affection for your own friends, relations, sons, grandsons, and wife. If you possess all these five qualities, even if you possess no others, you shall be the most excellent of men."

Zhönnu Loden said, "Even if one knows all these instructions, it will be difficult to apply them in practice. Nowadays, if you notice how most people talk, it seems that there is no one who is not gentle-mannered and learned. But if you watch what they're doing, it looks as though they are only people of crude behavior. So please tell me, what is the reason for this state of affairs?"

The old man said, "O, Zhönnu Loden, listen well and keep it in mind. The reason why people these days know but cannot practice is that they are overpowered by selfish motives and emotions.

Fools are clever when they watch,
But they don't know anything when it is entrusted to
their hands.

"So it is wrong to allow one's mind to be overpowered by defilements. If a person is overpowered by passion, he will steal the wealth of others or embezzle funds, snatch women, and get into lawsuits. He will destroy sacred objects, cheat friends, and take the lives of others. If he is overpowered by anger, he will beat and abuse his parents, harbor resentments, and tell the faults of friends. He will afflict himself and others with sorrow by beating, killing, and quarreling with everybody. If he is overpowered by pride, his mind will swell up with egotism and conceit, he will be contemptuous and mocking, repeat the faults of others, and feel hatred for inferiors. If he is overpowered by jealousy, he will slander and speak ill of superiors, rival and be envious of equals, and be unhappy because of the power, wealth, and position of others. If he is overpowered by avarice, he will not be able to part with wealth to make offerings or give help. He will not be able to give assistance or loans to others. The time will never come when he feels he has enough. He will not be able even to use his wealth for his own clothing or food. He is the real hungry ghost. If he is overpowered by ignorance, he will not know anything about how to accumulate virtues or purify evil deeds, what kind of work is good or bad, who is a good man or a bad man, and what to accept and what to reject; he will remain in confusion. In this way, the six defilements, the five poisons plus avarice, will bring him all the undesirable sufferings of this life and the next. Since he is not self-reliant, the defiled selfish motives, which are the root of all wrong actions according to both spiritual and worldly ethics, are free to have their way with him. Now, if you desire to enjoy happiness in this life and the next, don't keep talking about other's qualities, but watch yourself and examine your own mind. Correct your own nature and keep yourself on the right path. This is the entire means of achieving both spiritual and worldly accomplishments. O intelligent son, did you understand? Listen again:

Wealth is the cause of great gain and loss;
Generate merit by offering and giving, the meaningful purpose of wealth.
The human body, difficult to obtain, is only for this one time;
Keep the precepts of *upavasatha* and *upāsaḳa.*
Anger is the cause of taking rebirth in hell,
Put on the armor of patience.
Laziness will not achieve the aim of this life or the next;
Be diligent like the current of a river.
Distracted people waste their human life.
Devote yourself totally to meaningful virtues.
In order to know how to apply the two ethics,
Practice hearing, pondering, and meditation.
Arrogant people will never be satisfied,
Jealous people will never be happy,
Lustful people will never be content,
Angry people will never be harmonious,
Stingy people will never be replete,
Ignorant people will never succeed,
Deluded minds will never be at ease.
If there is less defiled emotion, there is less suffering;
When the defiled emotions have ceased, suffering will cease.
So it is excellent if you can do away with the enemy, emotional defilements,
Which are the source of all undesirable happenings.

Slowly the old man stood up. Zhönnu Loden was filled with heartfelt joy, happiness, and trust; and he said, prostrating himself and showing respect to the old man:

O! The man of the glorious period of time
Is like a mine of the Jewel of Sayings!
The gracious parents and the older generation
Are the heart of the gentle people.
Such an instruction like the heart's quintessence
I have never heard before.

Today by the grace of the learned old man
Advice has come to an orphan from his parents;
In the future, like a father to his son,
Please give instructions again and again.
Precious one, your graciousness is unrepayable,
May I see your happy face again and again!

The old man was amused, and with a kindly look he said, "Oh, ya, ya, dear boy! Stay well, all right?" And slowly he went on his way.

2

Holy Dharma Advice

A Drama in the Lotus Garden

Paltrul Rinpoche

> Oṃ Vajra Tīkṣṇa.
> Mañjuśrī, Wisdom-being,
> Who plants the victory banner of the Dharma,
> Renowned for auspiciousness, virtues, and fame,
> Auspiciousness of all the auspiciousnesses, please
> protect me.

At one time, blessed by the sole divinity, Water Lotus, touched by the feet of the Ascetic Lotus King, in the country inhabited by Tārā Pemo Yoginī herself, in the forest on the wide face of the mountain Lofty Lotus Peak, in the White Crystal Lotus Cave, like the rising moon, in that place there lived a Brahman boy known as Lotus Joy who came from the Flower Garden of the Northern Plain.

He was all-knowing, wandering everywhere, living anywhere, and harmonious with everyone. He was training in the activities of the Sons of the Victors [Bodhisattvas] known as the meditation of Lotuslike Stainlessness. He was meditating on the mind of enlightenment known as Passionless Water Lotus.

At that time, not far from that place, there was a garden called the Pleasure Garden of Lotus Heaps, a meadow flat as a mirror, surrounded by a wall of trees, a garden of blossoming lotuses, filled with tall lotuses with straight stems, blossoming lotuses with wide petals, ripe lotuses with many sweet anthers, well-arrayed lotuses with large petals, unripe lotuses with blooming sprouts, closed lotuses with folded petals, decayed lotuses with no pistils, emptied lotuses barren of pollen, worn-out lotuses with fallen petals, smiling lotuses exhibiting their pistils, hiding lotuses remaining in their coverings, and naturally ripened lotuses ready to bloom.

Among them, there were three extraordinary lotuses; full, ripened, and well-arrayed. Of those three, two were fully blossomed and one was especially full and well-arrayed, but they were enjoyed by no one.

Then, in that pleasure garden, there were many swarms of honeybees zooming and playing. In particular, a tiny golden honeybee named Wide Lotus Wings and a tiny turquoise honeybee named Sweet Lotus Voice lived together as mates. The golden honeybee possessed youth, vitality, a bright intellect, and a broad mind; not anxious for new friends, he had a relaxed nature and was generous. The turquoise bee was also greatly able to give, with a beneficial mind and a tender nature; devoted to Dharma, she had little deceit, envy, or jealousy. These two, with affection for each other, lived together with smiling faces, loving words, and a harmonious way of life. In confidence they shared their minds' wishes with each other. Wide Wings said:

Oh, how delightful is the flower of youth.
It is not painted by the brush strokes of the Creator of
 Prosperity [God],
But produced by the illusory display of virtuous deeds.
Is it not even able to compete with the gods within the
 gods' realms?

The glory of enjoyments is not accumulated by
 ourselves,
But it appears because of the power of former deeds.
The tender seats of flowers are not woven.
The tender touch is their own property from the
 beginning.
The sweetness of the pistil is not prepared.
This drink of one hundred tastes is an immortal
 nectar.

The glory of happiness and joy does not arise because of exertions.
It is accomplished naturally because of former accumulated merit.
If you can apply the mind's intention to the Dharma,
Then your own body is worthy to be called the body of freedom and endowments.
However, toward the state of those human beings accomplishing evil deeds,
Although they can speak and understand, it is not worthy to make aspirations.

O, listen, my delightful sweetheart.
Here, the flower garden is splendid,
The taste and nutriment of the sweet nectar is rich,
The swarms of harmonious-voiced bees are numerous.
But the glory of the summer months is momentary,
The numerous causes of death are sudden,
The changes of happiness and suffering are instantaneous,
The escort of the Lord of Death comes closer and closer.

If we waste our lives in the desire for happiness,
Then the happiness of this life will have no essence.
Concerning the distractions of the so-called engagement in samsaric activities,
There is no end, now and in the future.
Even if efforts are made for this life's living arrangements for a long time,
There is no essence if the life span becomes exhausted.
Even though the appearance of this flower garden is comfortable,
If we must separate, then there is no benefit.
Reflect on this meaning and resolve your mind.
My loving companion, let us follow the Dharma path.
My fortunate friend, I aspire to the holy Dharma.
My heart-friend, do you feel the same?

At this, Sweet Voice said:

Excellent, excellent; sweetheart, you are right!
Your heart-words, the support of my mind, are right,
The words of your heart poured as the essence of my heart
Are my heart's nectar of immortality.
It is not invited here from the land of the Gods.
The delightful flower garden of the land of men,
The wealth of the fortunate and harmonious bees,
Provides great joy because of previous deeds.

Although beautiful, it is impermanent, the character of saṃsāra.
Although prosperous, it is impermanent, the wealth of illusion.
Although enjoyed, it is dissatisfying, the deception of wealth.
Essenceless is the realm of saṃsāra.

As for you, put armor on your mind.
I also will draw the same picture in my heart.
How can we change our firm decision?
We, fortunate friends, will follow the path of Dharma.

Hoarded wealth has no essence.
Even though seeking it through efforts,
Wealth will be enjoyed by others.
Cherished retinues have no essence.
Although they are cared for with kindness, it becomes an invitation to animosity.
Constructed castles have no essence.
Although intended to be beneficial, they become the rolling stone that cuts off life.
Cultivated fields have no essence.
Although counted as excellent, they become the slaughterhouses of insects.

Yet we should proceed slowly.
Hurried activities will not reach their end.
Let us write these heart-promises in our hearts.

No one but ourselves has greater control over our own
minds.

At that time there was a sage known as the All-Accomplished One [Don-Kun Grub-Pa] who had a peaceful bearing, a loving heart, and especially delighted in serving beings. And he came to that land. The two bees arrived near him and bowed with respect. They offered the sweet tasting honey. Commencing with polite speech they prayed to him:

> O great holy sage! You are the regent of the Teacher [Buddha]. Therefore please give a teaching in accordance with the precepts of the Buddha. You are the torch of the doctrine, therefore please give an essential teaching on practice. You are a member of the noble community [Saṅgha], therefore please explain the way of life of the Buddha's sons. We also will follow after you, Holy One.

Having heard their prayer thus, the countenance of that great Sage glowed with the effulgence of his mind. He displayed the splendor of his body. He expressed the resonance of his speech, speaking the Dharma thus:

Homage to the Noble Holy One!
To the Protector, the God of the Gods,
The Excellent One among human beings, the Peerless
Guide who leads living beings,
The Excellent being born in the Śākyan race, I bow
down.
Please turn the minds of the beings of the six realms to
the Dharma.

O two bees, you who are related to me by previous
karma,[1]
If you seek the Dharma path from the heart, then
reflect on this meaning.
These are the precepts of the Buddha, so think about
their purpose.
This is the very essence of the Dharma, so keep it in
your minds.

Ema![2] Living beings of the six classes
From past times have wandered long in the realm of saṃsāra.
In the future there will be no exhaustion of the illusory appearances of karma and defilements.
For tens of millions of eons, beyond calculation,
It is difficult even to hear the names of the Three Jewels.
Therefore, to meet the Buddha's teachings is like seeing a star in daytime.

In this age, the Fourth Leader [Buddha], the son of Śuddhodhana,
The Excellent Leader, the Lord of Sages, came to this world.
He turned the three successive wheels of the Dharma.
The duration of the doctrine, the tenfold five-hundred-year period, has not yet become exhausted.
At this time, when one has the desire for seeking the Dharma path and
Possesses the favorable circumstances of being accepted by a virtuous friend [teacher],
If you do not seek the Dharma path from the heart,
In thc futurc you will not takc rcbirth in this kind of land.
Even hearing the name of the Three Jewels will be difficult.

Ema, worldly beings who wander within illusory appearances
Apprehend the essenceless composite phenomena as eternal.
However, the realm of the elements of the outer world is impermanent.
The lives of the living beings, the contained, are impermanent.
In between, the glory of the seasons and months is impermanent.
Even those holy beings, the Buddha and his sons, are impermanent.

Look at their demonstration of the way of entering cessation [nirvāṇa].
For the Master of Beings, the Lord of Brahmas, the greatest within existence [saṃsāra],
There is no need to say that they will be lassoed by the noose of the Lord of Death.
No one has certainty of when and where one will die.
There are many causes of death and very few causes of life.
Therefore, you should seek the Dharma path quickly,
Otherwise it is uncertain when the Lord of Death will arrive, and
All beings are certain to die like animals in a slaughterhouse.

Ema, after death one will not disappear,
But one will transmigrate and take birth in this realm of saṃsāra.
Wherever one is born there is no opportunity for happiness.
In the eighteen hell realms beings are tormented by the suffering of burning and freezing,
In the hungry-ghost realm by hunger and thirst, and in the animal realm by eating each other.
Human beings are tormented by short lives and demigods by fighting and struggling,
Gods by careless distraction, dying, and falling.
There is no happiness anywhere, but a pit of fire everywhere.
In birth and the succession of lives, beings wander, suffering continuously.
You must develop revulsion for the phenomena of cyclical existence.

Ema, happiness and suffering are created by karma.
Karma is the creator of all things, like a painter.
Karma ripens without being exhausted even after one hundred eons.
Karma produced by oneself will not change and will not be experienced by another.

Virtuous karma produces happiness and birth in high realms and liberation.
Unvirtuous karma produces suffering and rebirth in inferior realms and saṃsāra.
Even if the cause is small, it produces a great result.
The glory, prosperity, joy, and happiness of the gods, the high realms, and
The unbearable sufferings of hell, the inferior realms,
Are created by nothing else but one's own karma.
Therefore at all times and in all circumstances,
Establish recollection, mindfulness, and alertness as the basis.
Exert yourselves earnestly in the right way of accepting and rejecting causes and effects.

Ema, the excellent torch that guides one on the path of liberation,
The source of all the qualities, the virtuous friend [teacher],
Performs the actions of the actual Buddha in this dark age.
His compassion and graciousness are immeasurable, greater than that of the Buddhas.
If you do not have a perfect, virtuous friend,
Then you are like a blind man entering a path without a support.
Therefore, this wish-fulfilling gem, this wish-granting tree,
The holy master—first examine him and then take him as a teacher.
Finally learn his activities and thoughts, and unify your mind with his.

This kind of fortunate disciple will not fall under the control of the devil, and
He will obtain the excellent path pleasing to the Buddhas.

Ema, the abode of nirvāṇa, peace and bliss,
Is the Dharma, free from all the diseases of saṃsāra,

The total perfection of the exhaustion of suffering
together with its causes,
The holy city, liberated together with its
uncontaminated paths,
Fully filled with the riches of the Victors and the Sons
of the Victors, and
The place of delight for the Noble Ones, the Hearers,
and Self-enlightened Ones.
It is proper to seek this path of liberation.

Ema, the perpetual, infallible, holy protectors,
The peerless Precious Jewels possessing graciousness—
I am satisfied by seeking refuge in them.
It is proper for you also to seek refuge in them.
If you take refuge with belief and respect from the
heart,
There is no equal to the Three Jewels, infallible
throughout all time.
The Three Jewels are capable of protecting from the
sufferings of saṃsāra.
The merits of taking refuge are equal to the limits of
space.
In this life, the eight and sixteen fears, and so forth—
The complete mass of unfavorable evil—will be
removed.
In the next life, it is certain that you will be liberated
from
All the suffering of an inferior being revolving in the
inferior realms.
Therefore always remember the Triple Gem,
Go for refuge again and again, and recite prayers.

Ema, the trial of progress of the numerous Buddhas,
The sole path of progress of the Buddha's sons,
The peerless jewel, the excellent Mind of
Enlightenment,
With its aspects of aspiration and entering, please
develop.
From this you will obtain the name of the Son of the
Victors.

You will proceed from the path of bliss to the field of bliss.
Attainment of perfect, full Buddhahood is not far away.
The beings of the three worlds are your kind parents.
They are like a protectorless and friendless blind man wandering in a field.
Although desiring happiness they indulge in the causes of suffering.
By composing the mind in love and compassion for them,
Thinking to dispel the suffering of all beings by yourself,
Attire yourself in the armor of this great, inconceivable mind.
Meditate on the equality of self and others, the exchange of self with others, and the view that others are more dear than yourself.
Practice with exertion from the heart the four boundless states of mind, the six perfections, and the four means of attraction of disciples.
It is said that the complete activities of the Sons of the Victors
Are completed in the excellent path of the six perfections.
This perfect, excellent path, pleasing to the Buddhas,
Is the essence of the heart, so keep it in the center of your heart.

Ema, the duration of living in the dwelling of saṃsāra is long.
From beginningless time we have gravely accumulated evil deeds.
Therefore, by the application of the complete four powers [*sTobs-bZhi*],
If one does not cultivate this skillful means of confession of evil deeds and falls from the precepts,
It will be difficult to be liberated from the inferior realms of saṃsāra.

The sole body of all the Bliss-gone Buddhas,
According to the jewel method [tradition] condensing all the root and lineage Lamas;
Vajrasattva, white like the color of the conch shell and moon,
Seated upon a white lotus and moon with a smiling face:
If you visualize him and recite the hundred syllables according to the liturgy,
Then you will destroy all effects of evil deeds and falls from the precepts, and
Stir [empty] the depths of all the realms of hell.

Ema, Buddhahood is for those who have completed the accumulations of merit and wisdom.
There is no chance of accomplishment for those who have not completed the accumulations.
Therefore, as a skillful means, offer the collected assemblage of wealth and
The Buddha Lands manifested by mind.
Visualizing the triple thousand Nirmāṇakāya pure lands, the unexcelled Saṃbhogakāya pure lands, and
The ultimate nature Dharmakāya pure land;
With your body, wealth, and virtues of the three times,
Offer these to the divine Lama, to the Three Jewels, and to the three Bodies.
From this, merit will be completed and one's perceptions of Buddha fields will be perfected.
The minds of beings will be ripened and the merit will be infinite.
Therefore I accept the accumulations as the heart of the instructions.

Ema, from beginningless time, due to ignorance,
Beings wander in saṃsāra by apprehending that which is selfless to be the self.
Desire and hatred arise through clinging to the nonexistent body, assuming it to be the body.

Therefore, this cherished illusory body,
Dedicate as the substance of offering and giving without attachment.
In the form of nectar offer upward to the Three Jewels, and
Give downward to the beings of the six realms.
They will be satisfied and your dual accumulations will be perfected.
All your karmic debts will be paid, obstructing and harmful spirits will be satisfied, and obstructions will be pacified.
All substances of offerings manifested by mind and all necessary wealth,
Offer upward and give downward and dedicate the merit for the sake of all beings.
All phenomena are merely different varieties of thought.
So this merit is equal to giving your own body directly.
It establishes the habit of great generosity.
It completes the merit, purifies obscurations, and causes the realization of the clarity of the intermediate state.
It ransoms death and reverses sickness, obstructions, and harmful forces.
Therefore this is a skillful means for the accumulation of merit.

Ema, the embodiment of the Three Jewels possessing kindness,
The essence of all the Buddhas, the precious one,
The holder of the treasure of teachings of the three transmissions, the blessed one:
The supreme guide, the root Lama—pray to him or her.
If you visualize the Lama on the crown of your head or in the center of your heart,
The merit is equal to visualizing all the Bliss-gone Buddhas.

The blessings of the Lamas of the three transmissions will enter into your own mind.
The Lama's mind and your mind will mix inseparably and realization will arise.
Therefore, for the most excellent method of progress in realization of the ultimate nature,
Guru Yoga is the profound essence.
Receive the four initiations from the lights of the letters in the three places.
Establish the capacity for purifying the four obscurations,
Attaining the levels of four bodies and the level of Knowledge-holder of the four classes.
You will then attain the potential to practice the four paths and will restore the decay of the sacred vows.
All the phenomena of saṃsāra and nirvāṇa will arise as the play of the Lama.
For the time being unfavorable circumstances will be pacified and wishes fullfilled.
Ultimately in this life you will secure the reign of Dharmakāya.
Even if not, in the next life you will be reborn in the land of Lotus Light.
In that land, from progressing through the path of the four Knowledge-holders,
You will enter into the primordial sphere like an illusion.
You will serve the purposes of beings equal to the limits of space.
The appearances of bodies and wisdom will fill phenomenal existence.

Ema, these are the sole path of progress of all the Buddhas,
The oral precepts of the lineage of the Knowledge-holders of the three transmissions,
The condensation of the sutras of the eighty-four thousand sacred Dharmas are

The crucial essence of the instructions!
Even if one hundred learned ones and one thousand
saints should arrive,
There will be no one who teaches a more profound
Dharma than this.
This is the inner essence of the sacred Dharma nectar.
This is the main practice of the thousands of the
Saṅgha, the holy assemblage.
By whatever merits are obtained through preaching
and listening to this path,
May all the endless living beings,
Relying on this excellent path, in a single lifetime
Achieve fully perfected enlightenment.

After speaking thus, he gave blessings and said aspirations for the two bees. By wandering, he fulfilled the needs of living beings, of whoever saw, heard, remembered, or touched him. Then in the hermitage known as Medicinal Eye Drops he attained complete nirvāṇa in the state of no residue of body, like the exhaustion of the fuel of a fire.

Then, for a long time, the two bees followed their daily lives mostly in accordance with the teachings of the sage, but sometimes they played carelessly with attachment to the objects of desire. Once, while Sweet Voice was drinking the sweet essence of the flowers and Wide Wings was flying around in the sky, the light color of the sun suddenly faded. The shadow of the dark clouds fell on the ground. The flowers simultaneously closed their mouths. Sweet Voice was enclosed within the flower. Suffocating, filled with fear and unable to speak, she remained trapped within, uttering "Bub Bub Bub Bub." Wide Wings, also filled with fear and helplessness, landed at the foot of the flower. His heart suppressed by torments of suffering, he rolled on the ground and said:

Alas, alas, how fearful and scary!
Oh, Oh, what a sudden misfortune!
What to do, what to do with this cruel violence?
Which devil has arrived here so suddenly?

The enchanting disk of the sun in the sky,
who is the ferocious one who has covered it so suddenly?
The one-hundred-petaled flowers arrayed on the ground,
what bad circumstances have terminated their lives so suddenly?
My charming, sweetheart companion, where have you gone?
My tender, wide-winged, moving one, where have you gone?
My emitter of sweet songs, where have you gone?
My confidante of love, where have you gone?
My beautiful, smiling one, where have you gone?
My delightful, buzzing one, where have you gone?
My turquoise, fuzzed one with slanting glances, where have you gone?
My beautiful six-legged one, where have you gone?
My shining, spotted one, where have you gone?
My black, rich hair-knotted one, where have you gone?
Piece of my own heart, where have gone?
Wide Wing's inside is empty; what to do?
Get up, get up! Can you hear, beloved Sweet Voice?
If there is no answer to Wide Wing's plea,
Then my heart will be near to splitting in pieces.

O sudden dark cloud without pity,
what is this catastrophe for the innocent bees?
O gracious, wide, one-hundred-petaled flower,
don't you have any independence?

All-beneficial sun, master of compassion,
please don't remain behind the furious dark cloud.
Please send forth your light rays and heat of compassion.
If I were Vayabe [the wind] I would be joyous that
the storm was dispersing the furious black cloud.
If I were a two-legged human I would be happy
with the power to open one hundred wide flowers.

Alas, high sky, do you pay attention to
this kind of fate of the humble bee?
Please issue a command to the furious dark clouds.

Sweet Voice, Sweet Voice, essence of my heart,
Sweet Voice, Sweet Voice, vine of my heart,
Sweet Voice, Sweet Voice, loving companion,
Sweet Voice, Sweet Voice, my beloved goddess, alas,
alas!

Sad Wide Wings said this, rolling on the ground in total exhaustion. In that place, when she caught her breath a little bit, Sweet Voice was able slowly to utter a cry. From the middle of the flower she called out: "Wide Wings, Wide Wings." Then, Wide Wings became very happy, thinking that Sweet Voice had revived. He stood up quickly and, facing the flower closely, cried out, "Sweet Voice." At that time, Sweet Voice heard the crying voice of Wide Wings. She realized that she was trapped within the middle of the flower and considered the situation precisely. She thought:

"Oh no, although we two have formerly heard all the profound teachings from that Great Sage known as Accomplishing the Welfare of All, we have not practiced even a little. Although we made the promise and had the determination to practice the pure, holy Dharma, my life has become exhausted in the state of merely wishing to practice Dharma. Now I must die enclosed within the middle of this flower after having experienced for a long time suffering like the decline and fall of the gods. Or will it be possible that, being touched by the rays of the sun, the one-hundred-petaled flower will open and I will be delivered before death arrives? Either way, Wide Wings is depressed by sorrow and if I give an answer he might hear." She said:

O, O, Wide Wings, O, O, Wide Wings,
Excellent Wide Wings, divine prince,
After hearing your charming sweet voice, nectar of the
ears,
I have joy in my heart; but this youthful, handsome
face,

The nectar of the eyes, what a misfortune that I cannot
see it.

The sudden dark messenger of the Lord of Death,
I do not know when he will arrive.
Beneficial to all, the creator of the day, the orb of light,
Without remaining in the sky, where did it go?

The decorative bedding of petals, soft to the touch,
The dripping essence of nectar, sweet to the taste,
The ambrosia of the nose, sweetly fragrant to the smell,
The youthfulness of white and red flowers, the joyful
celebration for the eyes,
The assembly of flowers, the enjoyment of all wishes,
How did it become a murdering executioner?
The hundreds of thin, soft petals becoming a vicious
prison, and
The sweet wealth becoming binding chains
Is the character of the suffering of change.

O! When the great, kind sage
Gave the nectar-like instructions,
He said that impermanence was the characteristic of
saṃsāra.
Today it is apparent to us.
Although my enjoyments competed with the prosperity
of the gods,
To arrive exhausted at the gates of the Lord of Death
Did not take more than the blink of my eyes.
Alas, the suffering of death is like this.

Although I had in mind the desire to practice the
divine Dharma,
I was unable to immediately endeavor in practice.
If I must proceed on the long, narrow path of the
intermediate state,
I will not have any sacred Dharma attainment on
which to rely.

Although the thought of death's coming was in my
mind,

While being careless, indifferent, and lazy,
The demon Lord of Death has suddenly arrived.

Although I had in my mind the suffering of saṃsāra,
I could not cut off the attachment to the joys of adventitious appearances.
Through the five faculties being deceived by the five devils of the objects,
The basis of the suffering of saṃsāra has been established.
Although the belief in the infallibility of cause and effect was in my mind,
I could not practice their profound acceptance and rejection.
Having exhausted life in the state of distraction,
I have no reliance on the practice of virtue.

O my youthful sweetheart bee,
There is a fearful enemy, the Demon Lord of Death,
Of whom I have formerly heard.
Now he has arrived in person.

Regarding a dwelling place,
I don't have in my heart the desire to leave the flower garden,
But now suddenly by the Lordly King of Death
I am being led to the city gates of the Lord of Death.
Regarding food to eat,
Although in my mind I don't have the desire to abandon the sweet honey,
By the law of the powerful one, powerless,
I must eat the burnt smell as food.

Regarding the path of travel,
Except for the wide sky I don't have the desire to land anywhere else,
But now taken by the Lord of Death, powerless,
It seems necessary to wander on the narrow path of the intermediate state.

Regarding loving relations,
Although I don't want to separate from my gracious mother and father,

Now in the court of the King of the Law,
Relationless and friendless, it seems I must wander.

Regarding my cherished retinue, my friends the honeybees,
Although I don't wish to be separated from them,
Now from taking the great road of the next life,
Friendless and alone, it seems I must wander.

Regarding clothing to wear,
Although in my mind I don't wish to abandon the soft and tender cotton,
Now bound by the noose of the Lord of Death,
Naked without clothing it seems I am led.

Regarding my companion and friend, the golden bee Wide Wings,
Although in my mind I don't wish to separate from him,
Now due to the faults of compound phenomena being demonstrated,
It seems he will disappear from my sight and hearing.

O my handsome and youthful sweetheart,
From our first companionship to now,
Your beautiful face has been adorned with loving smiles.
I don't remember angry frowns.

Sweet Voice, cared for with words of love,
does not remember your giving wrathful scoldings.
Excellent nature of companionship with a loving heart,
I don't remember any shameless fickleness in you.

Regarding immediate wealth, necessities,
I don't remember your making distinctions between me and yourself.
For the long duration of our lives together I don't recall any unpleasant behavior.

The kindness of your caring for me
With a heart of excellent nature and loyalty is in my mind.

The affection of your companionship
Of uninterrupted love for me is in my mind.
The words of love of your enchanting and
Harmonious speech is in my mind.
The affectionate devotion of your
Ceaseless intimate heart is in my mind.

Although it seems I shall now be leaving my dwelling place,
I do not grieve from thinking about my land or my place.
Although it seems I shall now be separated from my amassed wealth,
I do not grieve from thinking about my abundance and wealth.
Although it seems that I shall now be separated from my cherished servants,
I do not grieve from thinking about my attending servants and deputies.
Although it seems I shall now be separated from my cherished body,
I do not grieve from thinking about my youthful age.
Although it seems that I shall be separated from my dear life,
I do not grieve from remembering the joy of this life.

But the suffering of inevitable separation
From you, my sweetheart cared for with love, pierces the heart.
There is no means to console my grief.
From remembering the beauty of your lovely face,
An incessant rain of tears falls from my eyes.
From remembering the attention of your loving heart,
The darkness of sorrow covers my mind.
From remembering the inspiration of your loving words,
The flame of sadness burns in my mind.

But what can I do? The forces of karma have arrived.
Who can repulse the forces of the Lord of Death?

Who can prevent the appearances of suffering saṃsāra?
You also, from thinking about this nature,
I beg you not to grieve.

Still, if the light rays of the sun arise,
There is the possibility of my being freed.
Please relax and remain optimistic.

Even if I cannot escape, and I die here,
There is nothing more you could have done in the past
Regarding loving care and affection, you, my heart-friend,
Who accompanied me with love. So the wishes of my life's end are fulfilled.

In the past when we were happy,
The promises of our wishes were written in our hearts.
Now do you remember in your heart, excellent one?
In the future even if the time of our separation arrives,
Please do not abandon your heart-vow.
If you could concentrate your mind and fulfill the training in holy Dharma,
There is nothing else to request from you than this.

Then Wide Wings said:

O Sweet Voice, O Sweet Voice,
Sweet Voice, my little singing turquoise bee,
Do not be afraid or fear but relax.
Do not be frightened or terrified but be courageous of mind.
Temporary situations do not last for a long time.
The dark clouds in the sky do not remain in one place.
It is impossible for the sun's light to fade.
The sudden dark clouds, this sudden unfortunate obstacle;
there may be a way to dispel it.

Our large circle of cherished insects, bees, and worms,
If we send them as messengers in all directions,
We will be able to accomplish the wishes sought by our hearts.

The treasure of honey, our accumulated wealth,
If we were able to give it as charity, would dispel our sudden disaster.
If we inquire from the wise and learned ones of the world,
We would know the means to avert the cause and conditions of our sudden disaster.
If we rely on others endowed with power and strength,
It would avert the face of the sudden dark cloud.

In unfixed nests in hamlets and rock mountains,
The small, black raven caws
And, it is said, gives predictions to the entire world.
If we ask him, he will give prophecies.

On the roofs of the lofty fortresses,
There is assembled a great flock of sparrows.
It is said that they recite the dhāraṇī of Vajra Vidāraṇa.
If we invite this flock they may perform propitiations.

In the midst of the wetness of ponds and springs,
There are frogs ugly in appearance.
It is said that they are messengers of black Māra Nāga.
If we ask them, they may have a way.

In the midst of leaves at the foot of trees and in holes,
There are black, venomous snakes revealing dreaded forms.
It is said that they possess the very form of the poisonous Lord of Water.
If we take refuge in them, the dark clouds will be averted.

In the abode of the mountaintop earthen burrows,
There are great, marmot meditators, meditating for a long time.
It is said that they possess the concentration to accomplish the absorptions.
If we ask them, they will grant heart blessings.

On the top of the branches of enchanting trees,
There are turquoise cuckoos emitting sweet songs.

It is said that they are the emissarial voices inviting the
rain clouds.
If we serve them they will silence their voices.

In the enchanting meadows of the northern plains,
Are the divine messengers, the small, wild, white-
muzzled horses.
It is said that they possess a jewel invoking the sun's
rays.
If we ask them, they will raise their muzzles.

In its own hole and in other uncertain places,
Is a nine-legged black spider, the killer of all.
It is said that he is the manifestation of a black Dolpa.
If we approach him, he will make arrangements.

From the sky, on the bare-rocked mountain tops,
Are brownish kites emitting screeches.
It is said that they are messengers of the King of
Eagles.
If we rely on them, they will show their wrathful
actions.

It is impossible to have a disaster that cannot be
overcome by some means.
It is impossible to have an evil deed that cannot be
cleansed by confession.
It is impossible to have an obstruction that cannot be
subdued by antidotes.
It is impossible to have a demonic obstruction without a
means of reversal.
The golden bee Wide Wings has ideas and methods.
In this spacious place I have complete independence.
I must try whichever of the hundred methods is better
and effective.

Having said this, Wide Wings approached the raven who said:

The source is the Nāga, the remedy is the Garuḍa.
The antidote is the wind, there are many methods of
reversal.

Although it is stormy now, there will be no ill effects
in the end.

Likewise Wide Wings visited all the others. The chief of the flock of sparrows said:

The blessings of this assemblage are like a force of
flames.
Since it is able to burn the forest of former evil deeds,
What need is there to mention a clump of adventitious
circumstances?
But careful offerings and services are necessary.

Having said this, the sparrow came and performed propitiations.

The frog said:

I, the frog, exhibiting ugliness,
Am the messenger of the Black Demon Nāga.
The barbarous Nāga is the source of the black cloud.
If I ask him, he will certainly be able to disperse it.

Having said this, the frog positioned himself, staring at the sky.

The serpent said:

From the fangs of the wrathful Lord of the Water
Arises steam, clouds, and hail.
Just as the snake possesses vicious fangs,
so I have the means to clear away the black cloud.

Having said this, the serpent slithered around.

The marmot said:

I contemplate on the absorptions without distraction.
But because the golden bee's presence is so compelling,
I will surely perform long-life prayers from my
meditation burrow.
It is certain that in the end there will be no harm.

Having said this, the marmot sat with half-closed eyes.

The cuckoo said:

The rainclouds are the emissaries of the gods.
Their messenger is the blue cuckoo.

> I have a little power over their movements.
> Of course I will do my best.

Having said this, the cuckoo sat flexing his body.

The wild horse said:

> I am the small, wild, grey stallion.
> My upper muzzle is the wish-fulfilling jewel.
> It is the broom clearing the covering of the sky.
> You did not make a mistake in coming to me.

Having said this, the wild horse raised his upper muzzle to the sky.

The black spider said:

> The breath of the vicious, barbarous Nāga
> Is not able to be cleared by other means.
> If the flesh of insects and flies is gathered,
> I will perform the offering liberating the harmful spirits.

Having said this, he weaved many threaded masts.

The kite said:

> I myself am the great Garuḍa, who subdues the Nāgas.
> I eat snakes, gobble up frogs, and destroy the wealth of the Nāgas.
> The power of my talons is like thunder.
> I will destroy the Nāgas into atoms by means of my wrathful actions.

Having spoken these words, the kite soared in the sky and screeched.

Then Wide Wings thought: "Judging from the explanations given by the great beings known to all, in the end the dark clouds will disappear and Sweet Voice will be liberated," and so he remained relaxed for a while. Then at that moment, the dark clouds started boiling and grimly churned in all directions. From the southern direction, the sound of thunder rumbled and the violent storm raged and howled. Simultaneously, the flower petals closed even more tightly. Enclosed within the flower, not only was Sweet Voice unable to move her arms and legs but she was suffocated and could hardly utter a sound. She said with a faint voice:

Kyema![3] Wide Wings, Divine Prince,
The hundred petals of the flower are tightening.
The roughness of the pistils is harsh like thorns.
The many furrows of the petals are as hard as a rock.

Enclosed, it is difficult to move my arms and legs.
Suffocating, it is difficult to inhale and exhale.
Choked up, it is difficult to speak.
Now it is certain that I shall not be freed.

From all sides the sound of thunder is rumbling.
The sudden storm is howling.
Since the flower is floating and bobbing,
The pond must be agitated and shaking.
It is certain that hail from the dark cloud will come.

When the violent hail arrives,
The growing green grass will be flattened,
The stems standing upright will break down,
The array of branches will be chopped off,
The ripened fruits will be scattered,
The blossoming flowers will be destroyed.

It will be almost as if the sky and earth are turned upside down.
It will be almost as if the hard rock is dismantled.
It will be almost as if the tall trees are destroyed.

Fierce lightning will come.
Now it is time even for you to run away.
Sweet Voice will not be freed, it is certain.
These are the last words of separation between the living and dying.
It is not proper to say much, but in brief:

The past words of the great sage,
They are sticking in my mind even more.
The words about the suffering of cyclical existence,
Now I recognize them even more.

The teaching about the impermanence of everything,
Now even more it has become manifest.
All that is gathered will certainly separate.
Do not allow your mind to be depressed,
I also will not grieve but will persevere.
Our past words, a silken knot,
Are they still tied without loosening?
Our wishes, pictures of stone,
Are they still vivid without fading?
Our promises, the stakes of the heart,
Are they still planted without being pulled out?

In the appearances of suffering cyclical existence,
Have you developed remorse from the depth of your heart?
In the uncertainty of the time of arrival of the Lord of Death,
Do you now have definite surety in your mind?
Toward the deception of the five sense objects,
Have you reversed attachment from the depth of your heart?
In the certainty of separation of all that is composite,
Have you attained firm confidence?

Though I met the holy lord [teacher],
I regret not having cleared away my doubts.
Though I heard the excellent teachings of the holy Dharma,
I regret not having gained experience in practice.
Though I obtained a birth having freedom and endowments,
I regret not having achieved the essence.

Though I understood impermanence and death,
I regret not having accomplished the Dharma for death.
Though I heard various aspects of causes and effects,
I regret not having been able to accept and reject them appropriately.
Though the suffering of saṃsāra was discoursed upon,

I regret not having given birth to remorse toward it.
Now death has suddenly arrived.

The frown of the Lord of Death is as black as darkness.
When his raging eyes dart about, I will be terrified.
When escorted in front by the fearful darkness,
Not finding my own way, I will be terrified.
When pursued from behind by the storm of karma,
Not obtaining freedom, I will be terrified.
When roaring like thunder, "Kill, Kill, Hit, Hit!"
Such delusory appearances arise, I will be terrified.

When the grimacing executioners of the Lord of Death
Perform their ferocious deeds, I will be terrified.
When my neck is caught by the lasso of the Lord of Death,
Powerlessly being dragged along, I will be terrified.
When transferring to the next life,
Friendless and alone, I will be terrified.

When I wander in a strange land without coming back,
Not knowing where to go, I will be terrified.
When the illusory appearances of the six realms are as clear as stars,
Without protection and refuge, I will be terrified.

I am an example of a person who intended to practice the Dharma
But was unable to accomplish it immediately.
You, my little sweetheart bee,
Contemplate on this situation and make efforts in the practice of the holy Dharma.

Without delaying, go to the holy Dharma.
Without wavering, commit your mind to practice.
Without deferring, bear courage in mind.
Without postponing, develop perseverance immediately.

Even facing significant difficulties, do not reject the Dharma.

Even at the cost of your life, keep your promise.
The counsels of this world are the words of demons.
Do not keep them in your mind but disregard them.
Distractions and laziness are the causes of deceiving.
Reject them as poison.

A life filled from beginning to end with Dharma,
A life connected to Dharma,
The practice of holy Dharma perfected to the end,
Maintaining security for yourself,
Achievement of the path of liberation for myself, and
Finally in the pure land of great bliss,
The direct meeting between living you and dead me:

Whether we accomplish all of this or not depends on
 you.
I will be counting on you from the next world.
My dead eyes will be watching you from the tomb.
My last testament is only these three [few] words.
Sweetheart, keep this meaning in your heart.
Now please, you should go to a mighty fortress [safe
 place].
Although I am going to the land of death,
It will be beneficial to my mind if you survive.
If you accomplish the holy Dharma it will be of benefit
 to both of us.
Before the arrival of the hail storm
It would be better to search quickly for a hiding place.

I make aspirations for your good health.
I make aspirations for your long life.
I make aspirations for your accomplishing the divine
 Dharma.
I make aspirations that you achieve your heart's wishes.
Now please stay well.

Having spoken, she suffocated. Then Wide Wings, tormented by the sorrow of the sharp thorns of suffering suddenly driving into his heart, unable to respond, remained and lamented: "A Kha Kha." At that time, from the midst of the gale, hail pelted down. From the sky above, the terrifying sound of thunder rumbled. The noose of lightning flashed in the sky. Wide Wings was stunned, and squeezing into a hole he continued lamenting: "Kye hud! Kye hud!"

Then the violent hail pelted down,
Landslides and floods seemed to fill the mountains and valleys.
Thunder and lighting seemed to fill the sky.
The crashing waves of all the rivers seemed to splash toward the sky.
All of the mountains became barren.
All of the flooded fields became dried river beds.
All of the lakes turned red as blood.
All of the large flowers, bushes, and grasses were flattened.

The small ones were scattered.
The long ones were broken.
The short ones were pressed flat.
The little ones were destroyed without a trace.

After that, as the dark clouds cleared away and the bright sun rose, Wide Wings went to the flower garden. All of the large flowers growing in the swamps and the fields had been flattened and scattered. The small ones had disappeared without a trace. All of the lotuses in the water, which were sunken into the depths when the hail fell upon them, now floated above the water when the hail stopped. The petals also opened and some bees pleasantly played and flew among them. The flower in which Sweet Voice was trapped had not been destroyed by the hail storm, but was sunk in the depths of the water, and Sweet Voice was dead by suffocation within it; her corpse stuck stiffly to the pistil.

Then Wide Wings' heart leapt to his throat, his eyes filled with tears, and he was weighed by great sorrow. The brightness of the sun, the blossoming of the flowers, the joyous play of the other bees, and so forth, all of which previously had produced joy in his mind, now became the source of more suffering. In a feeble voice he uttered lamentations:

How sad, how sad, how sad.
What suffering, what suffering, what suffering.
Suffering, the nature of saṃsāra, look at this, the miseries.
Impermanence, the city of illusion, look at this, the ruins.
Impermanence, the dwelling of illusion, look at this, how it collapses.
Unreal, the deceptive objects of enjoyment, look at this, how they change.

The flowers, well arranged in the past, their petals are destroyed now.
The plants grown in the past are everywhere flattened now.
The valley of joy and happiness this morning
Has met with suffering now.
The body and mind of my excellent mate of the past have separated now.

Wide Wings, cheerful in the past, has lost all hope now.
The objects of desire, attractive in the past,
Have become the source of suffering now.
The beautiful six-legged bee of this morning has become a corpse now.

From thinking about these appearances:
Sad, sad, my mind is sad.
Confused, confused, my mind is confused.
Disturbed, disturbed, my mind is disturbed.
Trembling, trembling, my mind is trembling.

The sudden devil, the Lord of Death, arrived for her first.
When will he come for me?
O Lama, O Lama!
Sad Wide Wings is sad!

For turning my mind toward the Dharma,
Lama, please bestow blessings.

Then the golden bee's mind became very sad, and, unable to stay, he went to the peak of the Lotus mountain. He flew among the turquoise junipers covered with dewdrops near the residence of the Brahman boy, Lotus Joy, and sang a song of lamentation:

Alas, it is delightful, the garden of flowers,
It is depressing, the city of suffering.
They are attractive, the five objects of desire,
It is repelling, the suffering of the formations.
My life-long mate, my charming sweetheart,
Has turned into an ugly, rotten corpse.

Please heed me, please heed me, O Three Jewels, please heed me.
I remember, I remember, now I remember the holy Dharma.
Quickly, quickly I will enter the path of Dharma.

Since all that is constructed will fall down,
What is the use of houses?
Since all that is accumulated will dwindle,
What is the use of material wealth?
Since all who are assembled will separate,
What is the use of relatives and loved ones?
Since all who rise will fall,
What is the use of position?
Since all who are born will die,
What is the use of the appearances of this world?

My loving companion, bound to me by karma,
About now she will have arrived at the land of the intermediate state.
At death, there is no hope other than the holy Dharma.

Since I have not practiced the beneficial holy Dharma myself,
Then even if I were rich, there would be nothing to be bought with wealth,
Even if I had many allies, there would be nothing to be taken by force,

Even if I were harmonious, there would be nothing with which to ransom my friend.
Even if I had virtuous karma,
Virtuous karma could not be sent as a farewell gift.

The law of the Lord of Death cannot be put off.
Without practicing there is no benefit from studying.
Without plowing there is no benefit from a field.
Without riding there is no benefit from a horse.
Because I now realize the uselessness of everything,
I will devote the rest of my life to the holy Dharma.

I will not think about enemies, nor try to subdue them.
I will not think about relatives, nor try to serve them.
I will not think about wealth, nor have time to accumulate it.
I will not think about leaders, nor show deference toward them.

I will not think about friends, nor be attached with affection.
I will not think about clothing, nor will I have warm and soft things.
I will not think about food, nor will I obtain tasty sweet food.
I will not think about houses, nor will I own dwellings.
I will not think about this life; the appearances of this life are demonic.
I will not think about anything; delusory appearances are enemies.

I will remain in the state free from conceptions, in openness.
I will relax in the state of no-thought, in contemplation.
The Realized One, the one who has seen the Dharmakāya in the state of nonmeditation and
Sleeps at the foot of the mountain, is joyous.

Since delusory appearances are dissolved, there are few discursive thoughts.

Since acceptance and rejection are dissolved, there are no efforts at fabrication.
Since hope and fear are dissolved, free from wishes,
The Dissolved One who is free from delusions is joyous.

The unmodified mind as such, the ordinary mind,
Unmodified hair, the freely flowing locks,
Unmodified actions, aimless and spontaneous—
one who is like this, the Ascetic [Yogi] who has renounced artifice, is joyous.

Since his inner heat burns, he is carefree in nakedness.
Since he has perfected his meditation, he is delighted without food.
Since he has realized self-awareness, he is at ease in nakedness.
The Adept [Siddha] who has perfected the signs of the path is joyous.

Since he has great perserverance, he is comfortable with austerities.
Since he is able to observe his vows, he dwells by himself.
Sustained by drinking water and eating pebbles,
The Sage who accomplishes his esoteric training is joyful.

Whoever practices Dharma is joyful,
Whoever is attached to this life suffers.
Among the solitary mountains it is always joyous.
The city of saṃsāra is suffering by all means.
Whoever relies on the Three Jewels is forever satisfied.
Whoever has hopes of profit and fame will always be impoverished.

I have paid and paid dues to my superior masters.
I am tired of paying them.
I will leave them to do what they like as they are.
I have given and given every gift to my inferior subordinates.
I am tired of giving to them.

I will leave them to do what they like.
I have protected and protected my mediocre relatives.
I am tired of protecting them.
I will leave them to do what they like.
I have fought and fought against my hateful enemies.
I am tired of fighting with them.
I will leave them to do what they like.
I have plowed and plowed my cultivated fields.
I am tired of plowing them.
I will leave them barren.
I have lived and lived in built-up fortresses.
I am tired of living in them.
I am going to leave for the solitary mountains.

I have eaten and eaten edible foods.
I am tired of eating.
I will enter into the ascetic life.
I have worn and worn wearable clothing.
I am tired of wearing them.
I will leap away in nakedness.
Now, I will practice and practice the practice of the
very holy Dharma!
Now, I will accomplish and accomplish the
accomplishment of the holy Dharma for death!
This is my vow. O Deities, please understand it!
This is my promise. My mind is the witness!

At that time, Lotus Joy thought: "Although the golden bee, Wide Wings, was formerly sincere toward the Dharma, reliable in all activities and good natured, at this time the sudden revulsion arisen in him due to circumstantial changes may not last a long time, so I must investigate it to test him." So he said:

O heart-friend, golden bee, Wide Wings,
Why are you lamenting alone?
Today your lifelong friend assigned by karma
Has suddenly been caught in the noose of the Lord of
Death.
However, don't feel sad but develop courage.

You should have the prosperity of worldly Dharma, the foundation of the holy Dharma
Worldly Dharma is the happiness and joy of saṃsāra.

What is the use of a Dharma that does not aspire to happiness and joy?
The purpose of understanding Dharma is desire for happiness and joy.

Even if one friend dies, how can you lack friends?
There is no example in the world of deprivation through the death of a friend.
The rotation of happiness and suffering is the nature of saṃsāra.
There will be hundreds of times when you think, "This is happiness."
The sudden renunciation of saṃsāra is the display of Radzas.[4]
It has no essence, don't you understand?

The sudden occurrences of faith are the changing shadows of the mind.
They don't last, don't you understand?
Vain generosity is Alahasud.[5]
It is fruitless, don't you understand?
Unfortunate circumstances are sudden, adventitious, and momentary.
There is no poverty or prosperity to them, don't you understand?
The combination of the worldly and Dharma systems is the thing to be accomplished by the wise ones.
In it is the path of liberation, don't you understand?
Transforming sensory objects into the path is the skillful means of Tantra.
In it is the short path of liberation, don't you understand?

Holding the position of a king is an activity of the Bodhisattvas.
In it are the benefits for beings, don't you understand?

For people who accumulate wealth, it is possible to give.
In it is the completion of the six perfections, don't you understand?
Many promises without the mind's determination
Should be known as the cause of many transgressions in the end.
Performing austerities without perserverance
Is the cause of the arising of wrong views in the end, so be careful!
Disgust and revulsion in saṃsāra, which does not endure,
Is the cause of losing the provisions of this life in the end, so be careful!
To stay in solitary mountains without having developed absorption
Is the cause of being fed up in the end, so be careful!
Without realizing the view, wandering in power [haunted] places
Is the cause of being possessed by gods and demons in the end, so be careful!
Without the attainment of accomplishment, performing esoteric activities
Is the cause of taking rebirth in hell in the end, so be careful!
Without changing one's own mind, to change costumes
Is the cause of others' feeling disgust for you in the end, so be careful!
Without examination, having many sporadic ideas
Is the cause of developing regret in the end, so be careful!
Without certainty in a single activity, to be involved in numerous activities
Is the cause of irritation of everyone in the end, so be careful!
Without obtaining the path of seeing, talking about foreknowledge
Is the cause of the impoverishment of self and others in the end, so be careful!

Without having developed compassion, acting for beings
Is the cause of the arising of attachment in the end, so be careful!

Without making subtle investigations carefully,
It is not proper to say whatever thoughts come to mind and
It is not proper to do whatever one has said.

After catching, it is essential not to lose.
After holding, it is essential not to let go.
Having spoken, it is essential not to lie.

O golden bee, keep this in your mind.
It is the heart-advice of the relaxed Lotus Joy.
These are the experiences of my own mind, please don't laugh at them.
These are loving confidences, please don't reprimand me.
Please keep it in mind and investigate it, it is the speech of truth.

The golden bee, a little displeased in his mind, responded:

Ema, in the solitary forest
The brahman boy is so relaxed.
Lotus Joy is charming.

To the tiny bee who is left alone,
Your consolation bespeaks your enduring friendship.
To Wide Wings who is lamenting,
Sharing confidential speech bespeaks your everlasting friendship.
To the golden bee who is tormented by sorrow,
Your giving consolation is a great kindness.
Your speech, which is harmonious with both systems, worldly and spiritual,
If it really possesses excellent meaning, then it is wonderful.

In the nature of samsaric suffering,
I, the little bee who has developed revulsion,

Formerly stayed with a holy teacher,
Concentrated my mind on the holy Dharma, and
Drew the promise of practice in my heart.
It is not just a sudden reaction, I swear upon death.

I kept the solitary forests in my heart.
I maintained the lives of the earlier masters in my mind.
It is not just childish thoughts, I swear upon death.

I focused my mind on the Triple Gem.
I carried the gracious Lama on the crown of my head.
There is no error in the object of my focus, I swear upon death.

I maintained a broad mind toward hated enemies.
I kept an enduring friendship with my loving relatives.
I don't hate or fight, I swear upon death.

I made offerings to the Triple Gem.
I gave charity to the disabled.
I did not give or offer fruitlessly, I swear upon death.

I kept my qualities inside [hidden].
I unfurled other's qualities like banners.
I did not have pride or talk nonsense, I swear upon death.

The enduring, lifelong friend
Has suddenly been caught by the noose of the Lord of Death.
This time I saw the impermanence clearly and
Developed revulsion and renunciation.
In my talk there is no pretension, I swear upon death.

I have written the promises in the core of my heart.
I have whipped my practice with the whip of diligence.
In these words there are no lies, I swear upon death.
Affable Lotus Joy, have you met the teachers who are true Buddhas, and
Do you posssess the profound instructions?
Have you carried out the studies, impartially pondered upon the scriptures, and

Have you dispelled the doubts about the words?
Have you observed your practices in solitary places, and
Have you developed uncontrived realization?
Have you sung joyful songs at the feet of rocky
  mountains, and
Has the power of meditative experiences blazed forth?
Have you performed your activities relaxedly and
  naturally, and
Attained the experience of equal taste as the path?
Have you seen the show of the cities of saṃsāra, and
Developed revulsion from the depth of your heart?

Please give a speech in accordance with the Dharma.
Please sing a song in accordance with the path.
Please give an example that illustrates impermanence.
Please denounce the city of saṃsāra.
Please speak of the virtues of the path of liberation.
Please speak the praises of the solitary mountains.

I, Wide Wings, the small golden bee,
Will make my residence in the solitary abodes.
I will maintain my affections toward the holy Dharma
  and friends.
I will watch the show of my own mind, and
I will have harmonious discussions with you.
I am presenting my words without any concealment.

Then the Brahman boy, Lotus Joy, thought: "The golden bee, Wide Wings, has a good nature, enduring friendship, and stands straight. He is not like many other ordinary beings who possess vanity and many sporadic ideas. Nevertheless, if I guess from what he is saying now, it seems that he has faith in the Dharma from the depth of his heart. So, I should speak to him in accordance with what suits his mind."

Kye Kye,[6] harmonious heart-friend,
You, Wide Wings, the golden bee!
You entrusted your mind to the Triple Gem.
You put your trust in the holy Dharma.

You reduced the scope of your thoughts
Through revulsion and renunciation, and
You have devotion toward practice.
These are the signs of having excellent aspirations in past lives.

You have understood the constructed phenomena
As impermanent and illusory apparitions.
You have developed revulsion toward the city of saṃsāra.
You have avoided the evil minds of this life's eight worldly Dharmas.
These are the signs that you have a karmic connection with the Dharma.

Your analysis has opened toward the objects of studying and pondering.
You have understood the acceptances and rejections of the profound causation [karma].
You know the activities of the Holy Sons of the Victors.
You have found the entrance to the excellent path.
These are the signs that you are accepted by a holy Lord.

To the fortunate little bee,
I, a disciple of an excellent Lama,
Give the introduction of the excellent certainty.
Accept it as an addition to your excellent intentions.

In the city of inferior saṃsāra,
The container [world] is called Māyā, the illusory appearances.
The contained [beings] are called solid delusions.
The container and contained are gathered together,
By frantically being involved in evil deeds.
Suffering is spread just as a fire spreads in the forest.

By having turned one's back on virtuous deeds,
Happiness and joy become like the stars of dawn.
By having embraced evil activities,
The age of dregs[7] draws near as the evening shadows of the mountains.

Within the grinder of the cruel hatred
Is marked the navel hole of desire.
In it is poured the popped barley of the humans of the upper realms.
Having been ground, it falls out in the depths of the inferior realms.

Watch the process of a few big grains at the top of the grinder.
Watch the process of the increase into many fine particles of flour at the bottom.
See the manner of how subtle the process of cause and result is!

In ancient times, in the Jambu continent of the human realm,
The towns were joined together breadthwise and lengthwise.
Roosters could travel from house to house by flying.
Wealth and happiness could compete with that of the gods.
The leaders were the Universal Kings.
They ruled their states by the power of their golden wheels.
The subjects were contained within the four continents and eight subcontinents.
The law was the ten virtuous deeds.
Human beings increased and migrated to the upper realms of the gods.
The gods increased and filled the flower gardens.

Nowadays, in the age of dregs,
The cities are lined-up broken walls.
The barren fields stretch out in chains.
The people eat meat and blood for enjoyment.
The leaders are the messengers of hell.
They rule their states by the power of war and death.
The subjects are wandering beings with evil karma.
The laws are based upon the means to get food and the spread of deception.

The endless roots of society are controlled by robbers.
The robbers are heading for the gates of the city of hell.
Their progress is the increase of the heat and cold of hell.
Their war is the victory of the demigods and Rākṣasas.
Their consumption is the development of sickness and plague.
The rulers, on their seats of power, defraud their subjects.
Through cunning they punish innocent people.
Through lies they enumerate the faults of their workers.
Through deceit they throw themselves and others into destitution.

The spiritual masters underneath their parasols deceive their disciples.
They employ the holy Dharma as a shield.
They roar their lies of foreknowledge with random guesses.
They perform empowerments as a business to accumulate wealth.
They pay attention to the dispositions of the worldly leaders.
For Dharma practice they perform ceremonies only to repulse the unfavorable circumstances of the townspeople.

The great meditators in their hermitages deceive their devotees.
In their hermitages they sleep like corpses.
If lay people see them, they straighten their bodily postures.
If they have wealth, they keep it hidden somewhere else.
To their patrons they express flattery.

The lay people deceive themselves.
Their minds are like a potter's wheel.

They look at what they want and then turn the wheel accordingly.
Their words are like the tools of a smith.
They are examined for their suitability and then altered accordingly.
Their activities are like the sky in the spring,
Now it is clear, now it is dark.
Lasting relationships are like the suckers of bees,
They are there while they suck, but absent when finished.
Flattering behavior is like a drawing of a thang-ka,
It is beautiful in front, but there is nothing behind it.
Affections are like a dish of lung,
There is something in the mouth, but nothing substantial [satisfying].

Religious people deceive others.
Their study and pondering is like the body of a tadpole,
The head is big but the tail is thin.
Their perseverance is like the mouth of a frog,
It is there when they hear but not when they practice.
They deceive their teachers with lies.
With cunning they craft the unspiritual into the spiritual.
With deceit they gossip about the practice of meditation.

When the earth is captured by robbers,
How can the highways of truth be maintained?
When the country is filled with fools,
To whom will the scriptures of the wise ones be taught?
When the rulers destroy their own laws,
In whom can the subjects depend through their happiness and sorrow?
When the spiritual teachers are only concerned for their own needs,
Who will work for the benefit of the weak?

When the leaders are robbing their servants and
retinues,
Who will take care of the destitute?

Alas, alas, alas!
In me, the young boy, revulsion has developed from the
depth of my heart.
Between the teeth of the Rākṣasas of impermanence,
The beings of the three realms are wandering.
Still bound by the attachment of apprehending
phenomena as permanent,
Having worked and worked for their necessities in this
life,
At the time of death they will struggle,
Grasping their hands to their chests because of
remorse.
They make sure to fulfill tomorrow's needs,
But they postpone the Dharma for the next life.
Look at how the bodies that were alive this morning
This evening are cold corpses.
Either tomorrow or the next life, do you know which
will come first?

I, the young boy, Lotus Joy,
Met the Lama, the real Buddha,
Who accepted me with a gracious mind.
My faith, devotion, and trust are one-pointed.
My devotion never wavered.
I said whatever arose in my mind.
I never made a choice about the terms that I used.
My activities are natural and spontaneous.
I have never deceived others nor am I two-tongued.
I have trust in one person and one deity.
I never sought refuge from others.
I spent a long time near holy teachers.
The number of the wise teachers I have had is many.
My impartial study of scriptures is vast.
Therefore I know what is Dharma and what just looks
like Dharma.

Little golden bee, Wide Wings,
If you want to practice the Dharma from the heart, and
If you have developed revulsion from the depth of your mind
You need certain teachings in order to reject various experiences.
At the beginning, when you seek the path of Dharma,
There are experiences that are similar to revulsion.
First is the revulsion caused by the languishing of a suffering person.
Second is adventitious circumstances.
Third is the abuse of lovers.
Fourth is the exhausting hardship of work.
Fifth is the interaction of elements in the body.
These are similar to revulsion but are not revulsion.

There are experiences that are similar to renunciation.
First is the renunciation caused by the desire for attractiveness by changing costumes.
Second is desiring relaxation in the comfort of a hermitage.
Third is to perform recitations with the hope of achieving esoteric powers.
Fourth is to make pilgrimages to see the world.
Fifth is the desire for the eight worldly dharmas[8] that create hope and fear.
These are similar to renunciation but are not renunciation.

There are ways of life that are similar to living in a hermitage.
First is to be strict outside and loose inside.
Second is to have no schedule and to be careless.
Third is to be involved in physical skills and sciences.
Fourth is to indulge in sudden works and activities.
Fifth is to waste the human life in sleep.
Even if you live in hermitages there is no essence.

There are experiences that are similar to disgust with saṃsāra.

First is the counseling of someone who cannot succeed in worldly dharmas.
Second is the sporadic speech of wild, crazy people who run around.
Third is the loud boasting of thoughtless people.
Fourth is the lack of concern for wealth of apathetic people.
Fifth is the sudden destitution of people who lack ideas for recovery.
These are similar to disgust with saṃsāra but are not disgust.

There are ways that are similar to wandering with renunciation in the world.
First is the way of those wishing to be excited by seeing sights.
Second is the way of those going to see pilgrimage places having no faith.
Third is the way of those doing circumambulations without knowing the benefits.
Fourth is the way of robbers who pick on others intending to rob them.
Fifth is the way of those rushing around without any thoughts.
These are similar to pilgrimage but are not pilgrimage.

There are ways that are similar to retreat.
First is performing recitations without visualizing the forms of deities.
Second is practicing the developmental and perfecting stages without certainty.
Third is doing wrathful practices wishing to attain power.
Fourth is completing the sessions of counting the numbers of recitations.
Fifth is practicing the four activities for the hopes of this life.
These are similar to retreat but have no essence.

Then, when you pursue the practice of Dharma,
There are practices that are similar to going for refuge.

First is the enumeration of the accumulation of words.
Second is not knowing how to rely on the Triple Gem with a trusting mind.
Third is not knowing the special distinctions of the objects of refuge.
Fourth is not knowing the virtues of the Triple Gem.
Fifth is going for refuge with expectations.
These are similar to going for refuge, but they have no essence.

There are practices that are similar to developing the mind of enlightenment [Bodhicitta].
First is the development of the mind of enlightenment, desiring good for oneself.
Second is expecting to have results and maturation.
Third is compassion with partiality.
Fourth is the development of the mind of enlightenment verbally.
Fifth is not to know, except for hearsay, about the disciplines of training.
Even though these are called the development of the mind of enlightenment, there is no essence.

There are practices that are similar to the developmental stage [*bsKyed-Rim*].
First is the pride of being the deity without clarity of the visualized form.
Second is the clarity of visualization without the pride.
Third is the doubts and hopes of the apprehending mind.
Fourth is the wrathfulness without the mind of enlightenment [Bodhicitta].
Fifth is the lacking of the applications of purification, perfection, and maturation.
Although it is called the development stage, it is the cause of saṃsāra.

There are practices that are similar to the perfection stage [*rDzogs-Rim*].
First is practice on the channels and energy without knowing luminous absorption [*A'od-gSal*].

Second is practice on dreams without perfecting them into illusions [*sGyu-Ma*].
Third is practice on the path of skillful means without liberating the knots of the channels.
Fourth is practice on the Great Seal [*Phyag-Ch'en*] and Great Perfection [*rDzogs-Pa Ch'en-Po*] without knowing the method of liberation.
Fifth is practice of Direct Approach [*Thod-rGal*] with attachment to the visions.
These are called great perfections, but there is no essence.

Lastly, when you attain the results of the practice,
There are results that are similar to acting for the benefit of others.
First is having foreknowledge of the appearance of meditative experiences.
Second is having certain accomplishments due to possession by gods and demons.
Third is giving teachings that accumulate the eight worldly dharmas.
Fourth is gathering retinues without leading them to Dharma.
Fifth is giving instructions, but having no experiences.
These are similar to the action of benefiting others but have no essence.

These fifty-five comparisons are not given as a mirror for looking at others' faults.
This is even refreshing for myself.
You should also keep it always in your mind.
When you practice Dharma just in appearance,
As to whether various kinds of deviations arise or not,
It is necessary to exert yourself in precise examination and correction.

Though my words have no great beauty,
The meaning possesses the taste and sustenance of nine innumerable profundities.
It is the oral transmission of the peerless Lama.

If you intend to practice the holy Dharma from the heart,
There is no need for gossip and boasting,
There is no need to prepare a show of provisions,
There is no need to fix a time,
There is no need to go away to seek Dharma.

The holy Dharma is like the body and its limbs.
Whenever you need it, it is within yourself.
Every instant you should exert yourself.
At all times you should clearly remind yourself.
In each moment you should correct yourself.
Every day you should reprimand yourself for your evil deeds.
Every morning you should make vows.
In every period of meditation you should analyze yourself.
Even incidentally, you should not separate yourself from Dharma.
In the stream of time you should not forget the Dharma.

If the practice is not performed in its subtlety,
Then for the practitioner who puts on a great show of practicing Dharma
It has no way of becoming a true form of Dharma.

First, carried off by laziness in the mountains;
Second, practicing in the monasteries with distractions;
Third, seeking solitude and desiring comforts;
In the world there is nothing worse than these three.
Divine Prince, do you follow?

Happiness is not good, suffering is good.
If you are happy, the five poisonous emotions rage.
If you suffer, previously accumulated evil deeds are exhausted.
Suffering is the kindness of the Lama.

Praise is not good, blame is good.
If praised, then pride and arrogance increase.

If blamed, then one's own faults are exposed
Defamation is the gift of the Gods.

High position is not good, a low position is good.
If you are high, pride and jealousy arise.
If you are low, openess and dedication increase.
A low position is the seat of superior ones.

Wealth is not good, poverty is good.
If you are wealthy, there is the great suffering of collecting and protecting.
If you are poor, austerity and the holy Dharma are accomplished.
The body [life] of a beggar is the goal of the religious person.

Being given to is not good, being stolen from is good.
If one is given to, then the load of karmic debt increases.
If one is stolen from, then the debts of future lives are paid back.
Contentment is the crown jewels [common wealth] of the Noble Ones.

Friends are not good, enemies are good.
Friends hinder the path of liberation.
Enemies are the objects of patience.
The practice of equal taste is the crucial juncture.

If you want to practice according to Dharma, you should act according to this advice.
If you want to make up your mind, you should act according to this advice.
If you want to live in a solitary retreat, you should act according to this advice.
If you want to roam around the world, you should act according to this advice.
The six condensed points, the essential profound advice, is the oral transmission of the sole father Guru.
These six words are the essence of the heart.

Except to you, my sole friend, I have not shown even a hint to others.

Ema, golden bee, divine prince!

For the sacred pilgrimage place to stay in, there is the high-peaked Lotus Mountain.
This is the pure land of the sole deity, Tārā.
This is the palace of Avalokiteśvara.[9]
This is the place of accomplishment of the Lotus King.
Look at this mountain, the body of the Noble One.
It possesses his complete form, relaxing in the natural state of mind.
Look at the rocks, the speech of the Noble One.
There are countless self-emerged six-syllable mantras.
Look at the trees, the blue-green groves.
They perfect the characteristics of the Land of Turquoise Leaves, the Pure Land of Tārā.
This land is surrounded by vicious, venomous snakes.
It is difficult for small-minded, ill-fortuned people to cross into it.
It possesses the characteristics of the Potala Mountain, the Pure Land of Avalokiteśvara.
In front is the heart emanation—the Lotus Born,
Sending forth emanations for the sake of beings.
Nearby is the beautiful palace of the women saints.
The time for these goddesses to serve beings has arrived.
In the heart of Avalokiteśvara is the meditation cave of me, Lotus Joy.

For the deity, we will accept the powerful Avalokiteśvara.
For the mantra, we will recite the six syllables.
For the Dharma, we will meditate on loving-kindness and compassion.
For the path, we will pursue the blissful path of the Sons of the Victors.
Then, even if we should desire suffering, we will experience only happiness!

Happiness for this life, joy for the next life—A-la-la [wonderful]!
We will proceed from happiness to happiness.
Eternal happiness will never change, A-la-la!
Let us make prayers to the Lord Lama.
His compassion will not fail, A-la-la!

Let us beseech Avalokiteśvara as our tutelary deity.
The accomplishments will not be postponed, A-la-la!
It is a great wonder!
Don't you think this is a great wonder, Divine Prince?

First, my heart vows;
Second, your heart wishes;
If they agree, then we will be able to follow after the lives of the past masters.
Let us renounce the path of the eight worldly dharmas like stones on the road,
Abandon the appearances of this life like harmful poison,
And practice subtly on diligence.
Let the instructions strike our own faults,
Let us throw boasting and gossiping to the wind.
Let us maintain our attitude along the path of Bodhicitta.
If we agree on these, then we have established the basis for counsel.
Two brotherly friends who have agreed in harmony
Proceed together along the path of liberation.
We are protected by these aspirations.
Throughout all successive lives we will meet together.
We will practice the Bodhisattva activities together.
Do you think this is proper, Divine Prince?
This is the condensation of the meanings, A-la-la!
This is the joining together of all the essential instructions.

When this had been said, Wide Wings agreed very much, and his wisdom was perfected.

As the moon waxes in the night sky of autumn,
The divine Mañjuśrī displays the signs and
characteristics of youth.
For the Buddhas, he is the wisdom-being.
For all beings, he is the ultimate nature of their minds.

For the realm of endless beings, the characteristic of
which is suffering,
The One with Unblinking Eyes [Avalokiteśvara]
stretches his long arms of loving-kindness.
For the Buddhas, he is the great compassion.
For all beings, he is their seed of liberation.

The holder of the profound treasure of mystery
Is the Holder of the Vajra [Vajrapāṇi], the master of the
mysteries of all the Buddhas.
For the Buddhas, he is their wisdom-actions.
For the realm of beings, he is the presence of the union
of naked intrinsic awareness and emptiness.

I pray to the Sons of the Victors, the Lords of the
Three Classes.
Lord Lama, who is inseparable from them, please
bestow your blessings.
Until the attainment of enlightenment I hold you as
the family Lord without separation.
O Compassionate Ones, please hold me continually
with compassion.

This speech, which is in accordance with the divine doctrine, known as the Dramatic Performance in the Lotus Garden, at the request of the boy Trashi Geleg, with his root points, is written by the relaxed Paltrul.

3

Beautiful Garland of Flowers

Advice on Two Ethics

Jigme Thrinle Özer

If you hold the triple gem as your refuge, all your wishes will be achieved.

If you see the spiritual guide [lama] on the crown of your head, all the blessings will enter you.

If you make offerings to the Dharma protectors, all the obstructions will be cleared.

If you appease the local spirits, the lords of nature, all the positive circumstances will arise.

If you adore your five physical energies, they will manifest as your benefactors.

If you pay tribute to the deities of wealth and luck, all kinds of prosperity will come to you.

If you serve your lords and ministers sincerely, they will extend their facilities to you.

If you respect your parents on the crown of your head, all will shower praise upon you.

If you earn the friendship of many people, your strength will be magnified.

If you build your friendship with powerful people, you will achieve your goals easily.

If you marry rich spouses, you will gain prosperity.

If you consult with elders, you will not have rotten ideas.

If you confer with all the people concerned, you won't face any accusations.

If you are skillful in analyzing projects, you will be successful in sorting them out.

If you refrain from jealous thoughts, your mind will be at ease.

If you keep others' treatment of you in mind, the time of needing revenge may come.

If you take care of your property, you will become wealthy.

If you have food, herds, and wealth, all will respect you.

If you abstain from cheating, pretending, and stealing, you will have friendship with all.

If you speak diplomatically, you will face fewer litigants.

If you have laughter and play with your family, they will become companions in joy.

If the ruler has no contentment, the nation will be at war.

If the ministers mislead the ruler, the national policy will plunge into turmoil.

If the ministers issue unfair judgments, the country will be destroyed.

If a monk involves himself in profit making, he loses his vow of discipline.

If a leader or master is harsh, it will be hard for any to serve him.

If a husband wanders too much, it will lead him to the law courts.

If a wife is too critical, she will alienate herself from everyone.

If a young son intrigues to punish others, he will be like a crop destroyed by a hailstorm.

If a daughter becomes old at her parents' home, she will become hateful to her mother.

If a husband interferes in home affairs, his wife will abandon him.

If a coward talks heroically, his friends will laugh at him.

If a weak person amasses too much wealth, he will lose it all to enemies.

If a childless couple amasses wealth, it will be possessed by the chieftain [government].

If a person with no training rides in a horse race, he will break his head.

If a scholar swells with pride, he has been caught in demonic traps.

If a rich person is miserly, he is hanging himself by the neck.

If a poor person spends carelessly, his enjoyment will be short-lived.

If a person of small merit prospers even a little, he talks arrogantly.

If an uncultured person is placed in too high a position, he has contempt for all.

If an inferior person is venerated, he seeks the high seat.

If you distance yourself from your parents, it will bring you ill repute.

If a servant is placed in higher authority, he threatens his master.

Do not settle in a rough location, because it brings fear.

Do not challenge Bandes and Bönpos as enemies, for it may cause curses.

Do not keep ill-fated substances at home, for you will suffer losses.

Do not dig out earth or rocks at sacred places, as it will bring ill effects from Nāgas.

Do not disturb the lords of nature and the land, as it may cause lightning and hailstorms.

Do not blurt out whatever crops up in your mind, as it may cause disharmony.

Do not wander without purpose, as it causes distractions.

Do not entertain unnecessary guests, as it only wastes food and wealth.

Do not lend to or invest with untrustworthy people, as it will be hard to be paid back.

Do not be paranoid, as it becomes the basis of harmful influences.

Do not push your relatives away as enemies, but win them as supporters.

Do not relinquish your friendship with neighbors, but enjoy entertainments together.

Do not distance yourself from common people, even if you are distinguished, as you might fall among commoners.

Do not take whatever you hear as true, but examine it.

Do not share your secrets as soon as you make friends, as one day you might be in dispute with them.

Do not defame someone as soon as you are in dispute, as one day you might be in concord with him.

Do not give away damaging proverbs to others, as you may need them for your own use.

Do not ridicule the food you get, as you may receive retribution.

Do not treat domestic animals harshly, as it diminishes the favor of the God of Luck.

Do not dwell in guilt over your past deeds, but abstain from repeating them.

Do not forfeit your wealth to others' control, but supervise it yourself.

Do not wear out your rich clothes at home, but wear them in gatherings.

Do not brag about your happiness, as it is not sure how long it will last.

Do not have contempt for the poor, as your turn to decline may come.

Remain in the company of people who are helpful and stable.

Follow the advice given to you by those who are kind to you.

Marry a spouse who is loving, cheerful, and joyful to keep company with.

Whatever projects you undertake, carry them out according to the circumstances of the time and place.

Do not trust anyone, until you know the person well.

Speak honestly to those who are honest as well as to those who trust in you.

With those people who are just testing you, be careful about sharing your intimacy and catching any social diseases.

Whatever projects you undertake, initiate them with favorable astrological indications.

Do not follow the advice of people who speak sweetly but have harsh minds.

Do not listen to servants who lie.

Do not commit even the slightest hint of deceitfulness to your heart-friends.

Do not challenge those enemies who are unconquerable.

Do not wait for those people who have gone for good.

Do not speak secrets in gatherings.

Do not use obscene language when high and moral individuals are present.

Do not sleep or travel at night in places where spirits are active.

Do not sit with people of gloomy face and poisonous heart.

Do not get involved in close relationships with ill-behaved and uncultured people.

Do not entrust a hard job to people who are unequipped for it.

Do not ask for confidential advice from a person who is not wise enough to give it.

Do not share words of advice with people who will not listen to them.

Do not show your admiration and smile at people who don't respect it.

Do not make wishes for the lives of people who are full of evil deeds.

Do not crave others' food and wealth.

Do not marry someone who has a bad reputation.

Do not live with people who are hot-tempered or have troubles with the law.

Do not buy things that are condemned or abandoned.

Do not swear by renouncing the Triple Gem.

Do not commit evil deeds, even for the sake of relatives.

Do not admire robbers or people who lead dark lives.

Do not deceive those people who rely on you and trust in you.

Do not exchange your eternal happiness for temporal joy.

Do not look for others' faults, but see your own faults.

Do not praise yourself and have contempt for others, but be realistic.

This dual ethical instruction entitled *Beautiful Garland of Flowers* is written by me, Jigme Thrinle Özer, at the time of my death, as advice for future followers.

4

Reminder to Son Śrī

Paltrul Rinpoche

There are three things that you should not forget:
Kind teachers, the compassionate Buddha, and recollections and mindfulness.

There are three things that you should remember:
The master who gave you the precepts, the scriptures that disclose the disciplines, and the disciplines to observe.

There are three things that you should place:
Your body in the seat, mind in the body, and relaxation in the mind.

There are three things that it is better to forget:
Enemies, who are the object of anger, the objects of desire, and sleepiness, which is ignorance.

There are three things that it is better to control:
Your mouth when you are at gatherings, your hand when you are alone, and your mind all the time.

There are three things that it is better to keep secret:
Sudden thoughts of emergence from saṃsāra, deceptive tricks, and sudden virtuous trainings.

There are three places where you should not go:
Among enemies, in gatherings, and to plays.

There are three things that you should not tell:
Dharma teachings to people who do not want to listen, your life story to people who are not close to you, and stories of impossible events.

There are three things that it is better not to have:
Sudden pleasant or angry tempers with friends, changes in your words, and differences in your actions according to the presence or absence of people concerned.

There are three things that you should not do:
Talking self-centeredly, talking behind others' backs, and expressing contempt for any person.

There are three things that you should not give away:
Wealth to high people, faith to fools, and heart-talks to anyone.

There are three things that you should not check:
The body of a beauty, projects of friends, and your own merits.

There are three things that should be in conformity:
Your talks with friends, clothes with the country, and mind with Dharma.

There are three things to which you should pay no attention:
Praise of yourself, the talk of new acquaintances, and the talk of unwise people.

There are three things to which you should not aspire:
The wealth of rich people, the positions of high people, and the ornaments of beautiful people.

There are three things that you should not condemn:
A person whom people love, things others are selling, and the people who are kind to you.

There are three kinds of people whom you should not praise:
A person whom people condemn, foolish egoistic people, and children who are uninformed.

There are three kinds of people whom you should neither praise nor condemn:
Your relatives, unknown lamas, and all unknown people.

There are many aspects, but in brief: Always look to yourself. Don't forget. Both Dharma and worldly ethics are condensed in that. It is the instruction in one word. It is very profound. This is the advice of Dri-me Lodro to his son Śrī, who is as dear as his own heart. Please practice it.

5

Instructional Advice on Training in Buddhism

Paltrul Rinpoche

O root lama, the great vajradhara, who is the
embodiment of
The triple refuges and all the Buddhas in reality,
Please always remain inseparably on the crown of my
head, and
Bestow blessings without separation from me in the
three times.

O friend who is devoted to Dharma from the heart,
You have requested me again and again with these
heartlike words:
"Please write and give us your heart-advice."
So I offer you this affectionate message from the heart.

The first entrance to the path of liberation from
saṃsāra
Depends on having a perfect Lama.
So, with proper devotion without changes,
To follow whatever he teaches is important.

However, in these days, the age of dregs,
There are many people who are attached to having
Lamas deceptively,
Cherishing the desires for this life in their hearts.
It is crucial to reverse such a manner.

Therefore, whatever is the essence of your wish,
Without concealing it, again and again
From the bottom of your heart

Recollecting it, you should speak to the Lama and implore him for the wish.

Although a gem is all wish-fulfilling,
If it is not anointed and displayed atop a victory banner
And prayed to, and aspirations are not made for the wishes,
A gem it may be, but no wishes will be fulfilled.

The Lama is the source of teachings,
But if there is no one who requests teachings,
There won't be any occasion for giving the profound teachings.
So it is important to request the sublime teaching, whichever one wishes.

Without practicing the teachings you were given earlier,
To keep yearning to receive further teachings
Is to do nothing but bother the Lama and provoke scoldings.
So it is crucial to exhort yourself in practice all the time.

You should do practice by knowing the crucial aspects of the teaching.
The essence of the teaching is Going for Refuge and Development of the Mind of Enlightenment.
Through these two one accomplishes Buddhahood.
There is no need to yearn for many other so-called profundities.

If the Fourfold Turning of the Mind to Dharma, the entrance to Dharma,
Is not born in the stream of your mind perfectly,
Even to hear other teachings is only to waste them.
So it is crucial to exhort yourself to tame your mind-stream.

Those people who don't eat what is given and who steal what is preserved,

Who abandon the Dharma teachings that they have studied
But pretend to be practicing something else,
Are doing nothing but causing others to be indifferent to Dharma and breaking the sacred pledge.
Without taming one's mind through mental disciplines,
The practices of body and speech do not benefit the mind.
Therefore it is crucial to contemplate with your mind again and again
The Fourfold Turning of the Mind and the Development of the Mind of Enlightenment.

If these contemplations are perfectly born in your mind,
And if your mind has entered into the Dharma without wavering,
Then the excellent Lama gradually will give you
The entire profound instructions of higher and higher teachings.

From the Difficulty of Obtaining Fortunate Human Birth
Up to the Development Stage, the Perfection Stage, the practices on
Channels, Energy, and Heat of the esoteric path,
And the training on Cutting Through of Great Perfection, which is the direct approach—
There is no Dharma that is not included in this.

Therefore, besides the teachings you have already received,
There is no need to request more.
However, it is crucial to receive clarifications and refinements
To resolve any doubts on the teachings you have received.
Having trained in the Fivefold Hundred Thousand practice, such as Going for Refuge,

To complete the Guru Yoga, the esoteric path of devotion,
With recitation of the mantra ten million times
Is the tradition of this lineage.

So if you have completed just the Preliminary Practice
Properly as it is and thoroughly,
Hereafter the certainty of your birth in Zangdog Palri
Is promised. See the instruction texts.

The unmodified, self-aware, and ordinary mind,
Which is thorough, free, and innate, is the Dharmakāya.
Realize that suchness of the mind nakedly
And maintain the thoughts, the appearing power of the awareness as liberation-at-arising.

Apart from this, some crucial points on meditation
I have given you again and again in the past, as you asked.
As there is no teaching higher than that to give you,
Please do practice on those instructions.

Thus, having been urged by a friend, who lives in accordance with the Dharma,
This is written by that shallow wanderer.
Although lacking in definitiveness, profundity, or excellent meaning,
It is an honest and direct message from the heart.

By the merits of writing this, in all the successive lives,
In the presence of the consorts of the Lord of Accomplished Ones,
In the single assembly, without separation,
I pray, may we be reborn and taste the joy of Dharma.

Thus, as prayed by Paltrul, may all be auspicious and may all be virtuous.

6

A Letter of Spiritual Advice

Lauthang Tulku

At the feet of the manifestation of the Supreme Deity
of Excellent Speech [Mañjuśrī], in the form of a
saffron-robed one,
Benefiting hundreds of thousands of wise beings, in the
garden of delight,
A blossoming white lotus of marvelous virtues,
The excellent incarnation Dönkun Drubpa [Thondup],
I proclaim this melodious, lutelike message as my gift;
I, who have opened experienced eyes on the Buddha's
doctrine,
Obtained learned ones' lotus-feet as my crown jewel,
And whose throat's roar of songs of scripture and
reasoning is not weak.

You, protector of beings, reached supreme attainment,
Perfectly endowed with the treasure—the jewels of
Freedom and Realization—yet
You are zestful in the beneficial intention to lead many
beings
Along the blissful path that you yourself have realized.
Therefore amid the possessor of wealth [the earth],
The tree of excellent signs [your body] bears good fruit
of happiness and benefits,
Displaying garlands of glory, while
The cool shade of your beneficial activities spans the
length and breadth of the earth.

I am fortunate that my head-cakra is adorned
With the dust of your feet, a crown gem

That, even for Brahmā and other gods endowed with the power of virtues,
Is difficult to obtain as their own crown ornament.

Through your presence, essence of all protectors,
I hope that the blessings of the sun—exoteric and esoteric doctrines—
Will for us, in the time of the Buddha, arrive in the Himalayan sky
By the power of the seven mares [the wind] of study and practice.

Various teachings, fresh garlands of blue lotus,
Colorfully fill the vast land of disciples.
However, the essential points of all these paths are as perfect as the taste of honey.
I honor you for remaining in the world, bestowing the essence of your intellect [the teachings].

Boasting that my residence, a monastery like a dried-up well,
Is a religious seat equal to Lake Manasarovar,
I am like a tiny fish, flickering with the antics of worldly activities,
Not yet caught in the beak of the water bird, the master of death.
The seal of prophecy as the wisdom-manifestation
Of the truly famed Lord Lama, the protector Mañjuśrī,
Is indelibly stamped upon you:
Please assume the mighty responsibility of study, debate, and teaching.

Please drink with your wisdom at one gulp in a moment
The ocean of numerous scriptures and traditions of the Buddha.
With marvelous fame of scholarship reaching out in all directions,
Grant new wonders to all who practice Dharma.

Although you possess many virtues, seek other virtuous friends [teachers].

Although in high position, think of common people as
your children.
Although honor and prosperity increase, cast your
worldly activities to the wind.
Observe how the Buddhadharma has come to a point
like the setting sun.

Kindly demonstrate the excellent tradition of
Practicing pure discipline, the root of virtues,
Stabilizing contemplation to prevent the inner
[subjective] and external [objective] causes of
distraction, and
Realizing the essential view of Insight Yoga, as an
example of the Doctrine.

There are many who bear the excellent vessel of the
acclaim of being great
With very little content of study, pondering, and
meditation, and who are
Wrapped in the ornamental cloth of noisy fame.
For you to lead such a life is inappropriate.

To be too affectionate to ordinary people,
To believe in deceivers, and,
Disregarding one's own faults, to praise oneself and
condemn others are
Not qualities of a holy person; so please be very careful.

There are so-called ascetics who treat offered material
as their ultimate wealth;
Loose people who just run from door to door to
perform rituals to earn wealth, and
Who with selfish intent pretend to act beneficially for
others:
Please never follow the example of such people, who
are merely imitators of ascetics.

In the *Mañjuśrīmūlakalpa*, the Lord of Śākyas [Buddha]
Prophesied the Buddha-deeds of
The Lord of Conquerors from the Tsong valley.
In your stable mind please preserve without loss the
essence of his teachings.

Here some foolish people, boasting of their knowledge,
Run after others' wrong views, and some accompany them.
As in the story of Chal,[1] it is their own silliness, and
The fault of lacking confidence in the teachings.

The precious share of teachings
Kindly given again and again by the Lama, one's own perpetual guide;
To abandon it and take up spurious texts
Causes the wise ones to be disgusted.

Therefore, uncertainty of one's own principles, like Kusha grass
Beaten down by storms, should be completely rejected.
Be like a nugget of gold toward others' rantings.
It is better not to believe them but to remain constant.

Complete the essential points of the doctrine, the core of the Buddha's vision,
The unerring tradition of the great Chariots,
The condensed quintessence of practice—"The Stages of the Path"—
It is the practice of your previous incarnation. So please practice it.

So-called high realization without study
Is like children running after rainbows.
When analyzed through scripture and reasoning,
Most of them are found to have fallen into wrong, narrow paths.

First complete the studies on the texts of "The Collected Elementary Topics," "Science of Intellect," "Science of Reasoning," and "The Five Texts."
Then the commentary on the discipline [śīla] chapter of *Bodhisattvabhūmi,*
And after that the "Fifty Verses on Having a Teacher" and texts on tantric precepts.
The commentary on the "Five Stages" of *Guhyasamāja*,

a text containing the meaning of the Empowerments and Development Stage;
After that, the tantras of *Vajrabhairava, Cakrasaṃvara,* and *Kālacakra,*
Followed by *Guhyagarbhamāyājāla,* and
Finally, conclude with the sacred introduction of *Dzogpa Chenpo* [*Mahāsandhi*].
This is the practice of the Omniscient Noble Lama, your previous incarnation.

You, who are praised as the incarnation of the Lama,
Develop the tradition of your last incarnation without decline.
By combined study and practice, like lions joining back to back,
To make your life meaningful is most essential.

At present you are young and intelligent.
It is time to act [study and practice] vigorously without making excuses.
The passing away of even a single day brings on old age, the end of life.
Wasting months and years in wandering is sad.

A person who couldn't apply the teachings of the Lama to his mind, and
To whom good and bad thoughts and efforts have been like the steps of a weaver,
A person like me, how can he offer you any advice?
It is just a plea from my own faulty mind.

Nevertheless, picked by the hand of perfect intention,
These water-born flowers of ethical sayings on acceptance and rejection,
I offer as a rain of offerings in front of you, the supreme object.
Please accept them with your compassionate mind and enjoy them.

For the successive future lives until the attainment of Enlightenment

I depend on you as the Lord of my Buddha-family.
From you, the protector, I request guidance,
At the time of the fearful intermediate state, the
separation of body and mind.
By the power of the divine, immortal Triple Gem
For the benefit of the doctrine and beings, on the
throne of Dharma may your lotus-feet
Be stable for hundreds of eons, and by turning the
wheel of the Three Yānas
Please may you generate the virtuous thought of
spreading the celebration of joy.

This is offered with respect by Lobzang Thupten Lungtog Gyatsho [Blo-bZang Lung-rTogs rGya-mTsho], known as Lauthang Tulku, a monk student of Grub-gar [Grub sGar, i.e., Dodrup Chen monastery], with gifts.

7

Instructions on Turning Happiness and Suffering into the Path of Enlightenment

Jigme Tenpe Nyima

Homage to Ārya-avalokiteśvara through the recollection of his virtues, which are celebrated thus[1]:

> He who is always happy
> because of the happiness of others,
> And extremely distressed by the sufferings of others,
> Who has achieved the quality of great compassion—
> He renounces caring about his own happiness and suffering.[2]

I am going to write a brief instruction on accepting happiness and suffering as the path of enlightenment. It is the most priceless teaching in the world and a useful tool for a spiritual life.

THE WAY OF ACCEPTING SUFFERING AS THE PATH TO ENLIGHTENMENT

BY MEANS OF RELATIVE TRUTH [*Kun-rDzob*]

Whenever affliction [*'Tshe-Ba*] comes to you from beings or inanimate objects, if your mind gets used to [*Goms-Pa*] perceiving [*'Du-Shes*] only the suffering or the negative aspects, then even from a small negative incident great mental pain will cause of bringing you unhappiness, and happiness will never have a chance to arise. If you do not realize that the fault [*Lan*] lies with your own mind's way of gaining experience, and if you blame external conditions alone, then the ceaseless flame of negative deeds [*ḳarma*] such as hatred and suffering will increase. That is called: "All appearances arising in the form of enemies."

You should thoroughly understand that the reason living beings of the age of dregs are afflicted by suffering is fundamentally related to the weakness of their discriminative mind [*So-Sor rTog-Pa*].

Thus, being invincible against obstacles such as enemies, illnesses, and harmful spirits does not mean that you can drive them away so that they will not recur. Rather, it means that they will not be able to arise as obstacles to the pursuit of the path of enlightenment. In order to succeed in using suffering as the support of the path, you should train yourself in the following two ways:

Reject the State of Mind of Exclusively Desiring Not to Have Suffering

Develop again and again the conviction [*Nges-Pa*] that it is useless and harmful to feel anxiety[3] and to dislike [*Mi-dGa'-Ba*] suffering by regarding it as totally unfavorable. Then, again and again with strong determination, think, "From now on, whatever suffering comes, I shall not be anxious," and gain experience of that.

1. The Uselessness of Considering Suffering as Something Unfavorable

If you can remedy [*bChos*] the suffering, then you don't need to be unhappy. If you cannot remedy it, then there is no benefit to being unhappy.

2. The Great Harm of Considering Suffering as Something Unfavorable

If you do not feel anxious, your strength of mind can help you to bear even great sufferings easily. They will feel light and insubstantial, like cotton. But anxiety will make even small sufferings intolerable

For example, while you are thinking of a beautiful girl, even if you try to get rid of desire, you will only be burnt out. Similarly, if you concentrate on the painful characteristics of suffering, you will not be able to develop tolerance for it. So, as it is said in the "Instructions on Sealing the Doors of the Sense Faculties," your mind should not fasten on the negative characteristics of suffering; instead, you should gain experience in keeping your mind in its normal condition [*rNal-Du bZhag*] and remaining in its own state [*Rang-So gZung*].[4]

Developing the Attitude of Being Happy [dGa'-Ba] That Suffering Arises

This is the practice of cultivating joy when suffering arises by regarding it as a support to the path of enlightenment. To apply this practice to your life, whenever suffering arises, you must have a training in a virtuous practice [*dGe-sByor*] according to the ability of your mind. Otherwise, if, having merely a theoretical understanding, you think, "If I have certain skillful means [*Thabs-mKhas*] to apply, the sufferings could bring this or that benefit," it will be difficult for you to achieve the goal. For, as it is said, "The goal is farther than the sky from the earth."

1. Suffering as the Support of Training in the Mind of Emergence from Saṃsāra [*Nges-'Byung*]

Think, "As long as I am wandering powerlessly in *saṃsāra,* the arising of suffering is not an injustice, but is the nature of my being in saṃsāra." Develop revulsion [*sKyo-Ba*] toward saṃsāra by thinking, "If it is difficult for me to bear even the little sufferings of the happy realms,[5] then how can I bear the sufferings of the lower realms? Alas, saṃsāra is an endless and bottomless ocean of suffering." With these thoughts, turn your mind to liberation [*Thar-Ba*].

2. Suffering as the Support of Training in Taking Refuge [*sKyabs-'Gro*]

Train in taking refuge by developing a strong belief and thinking, "The Three Precious Jewels [*dKon-mCh'og gSum*] are the only unbetraying refuges for those endangered by these kinds of fears throughout their succession of lives. From now on I will always depend on the refuges and will never renounce them in any circumstances!"

3. Suffering as the Support of Training in Overcoming Pride [*Dregs-Pa*]

Eliminate your pride and contempt for others, which are inimical to gaining any merit, by realizing, as discussed earlier, that you don't have any control over your own destiny and that you have not transcended the enslavement of suffering.

4. Suffering as the Support for Purification of Unvirtuous Deeds [*sDig-Pa sByang-Ba*]

Think carefully, "The sufferings I have experienced and other sufferings that are more unimaginably numerous and severe than those I have experienced are all solely the results of unvirtuous deeds." Think carefully about this with regard to the four following aspects:

The certainty of the process of *karma*

The tendency of *karma* to increase greatly

That you will not encounter the result of what you have not done

That the effects of what you have done will not be wasted

You should also think, "If I do not want suffering I should renounce the cause of suffering, which is unvirtuous deeds." In this way purify your previously accumulated unvirtuous deeds by means of the four forces [*sTobs-bZhi*][6] and try to refrain[7] from committing them again in the future.

5. Suffering as the Support for Attraction to Virtue [*dGe-Ba La dGa'-Ba*]

Think long and carefully, "If I desire happiness, the opposite of suffering, I should try to practice its cause, which is virtue"; and practice virtuous deeds through various means.

6. Suffering as the Support for Training in Compassion [*sNying-rJe*]

Think about other living things, who are also tortured by as much, if not more, pain as you are and train yourself by thinking, "How good it would be if they, too, became free from all the sufferings!"

By this method of thinking, you will also understand the way of practicing loving-kindness [*Byams-Pa*], which is the intention[8] to help those who are bereft of happiness.

7. Taking Suffering as the Support of the Meditation That Others Are Dearer Than Oneself [*bDag-Bas gZhan-gChes*]

Think, "The reason I am not free from suffering is that I have been caring only about myself [*Rang gChes-Par bZung*] from beginningless time. Now I should practice caring only about others, the source of virtue and happiness."

Conclusion

It is very difficult to practice "Taking Suffering as the Path of Enlightenment" when you actually come face to face with difficult situations. So it is important to become familiar [*'Dris-Pa*] in advance with the trainings of virtue that are to be applied when unfavorable circumstances arise. Also, it makes a great difference if you apply a training in which you have clear experience.

Furthermore, it is not enough merely for suffering to become the support of virtuous training itself. You have to realize [*Ngo-Shes*] that the suffering has actually become the support of the path, and then you must feel a strong and stable stream of joy [bliss, *dGa-Ba*], which is brought about by that realization.

For any of the foregoing categories of training you should think, "Just as the suffering I have undergone in the past has greatly helped me achieve happiness in many significent forms, the joy of high realms, and liberation from saṃsāra, which are all difficult to obtain, so too the suffering I am now undergoing will also continue to help me to attain these same results. So, even if my suffering is severe it is supremely agreeable. It is like 'Ladu[9] of molasses mixed with cardamom and pepper." Think about this again and again and cultivate the experience of bliss [peace, *bDe-Ba*] of the mind.

By training in this way, the overwhelming nature or superabundance of mental bliss makes the sufferings of the sense faculties as if they were imperceptible. Thus, having a mind which cannot be hurt [*gNod*] by suffering is the characteristic [*Tshad*] of those who overcome illness by tolerance. It should be noted that, according to this reasoning, this would also be the characteristic of those who overcome other obstacles as well, such as antagonists and evil spirits.

As mentioned above, the "Reversing of the Thought of Dislike for Suffering" is the foundation of "Turning Suffering into the Path of Enlightenment" because, while your mind is disturbed and your courage [cheerfulness, *Sro*] is extinguished by anxiety [*bZe-Re*], you will not be able to turn your suffering into the path.

Also, by training in the actual "Taking Suffering as the Path of Enlightenment" you will improve the previous training, that is, the "Reversing of the Thought of Dislike for Suffering," because, as you actually experience an increase in virtues through suffering, you will grow increasingly courageous or cheerful [*sPro-Ba*].

It is said:

> If you gradually train yourself through small sufferings, "by easy, gradual stages," as the saying goes, you will ultimately be able to train yourself in great sufferings also.

So, according to this instruction, you should train gradually because it will be difficult for you to gain any experience beyond the scope of your present mental capacity.

In the intervals of meditation periods [*Thun-mTshams*] you should pray to the Unexcelled Three Precious Jewels [*Bla-Ma dKon-mCh'og gSum*] so that you will be able to turn suffering into the path. Then, when your mental strength has grown a little, make offerings to the Three Precious Jewels and Spirits [*'Byung-Po*] and implore [*'Ch'ol*] them, saying: "In order that I may gain strength in the practice of virtuous trainings, please send me unfavorable circumstances." You should maintain the confidence of blissfulness and cheerfulness [*dGa'-sPro*] on all occasions.

When you are first learning this training it is important to keep mundane diversions [*'Du-'Dzi*] at a distance. For in the midst of such diversions you may become susceptible to the many negative influences of your companions' asking you, "How can you bear suffering and contempt?" The flurry of worries caused by adversaries, relatives, and wealth could defile and disturb your mind beyond control and cause bad habits. There are also various other distracting[10] circumstances that could overpower your mind.

In solitary places [*dBen-Pa'i gNas*], where these distractions are not present, the mind will be very clear [*Dvangs*]. So it will be easy to concentrate on virtuous trainings.

For this reason, even the Chö practitioners, when meditating on Stepping on or Controlling Suffering [*sDug-bsNgal Thog-rDzis*], at first avoid practicing near the harmful actions of men or amid worldly diversions. Instead, they train mainly with the apparitions [*Ch'o-'Phrul*] of gods [positive spirits] and demons [negative spirits] in solitary cemeteries and power spots [*gNyan-Sa*].

In brief, you should prevent attitudes of dislike toward internal illness, external antagonists, evil spirits, and unharmonious speech from arising, not only in order to make your mind impervious to misfortune and suffering, but also to bring bliss [peace, *bDe-Ba*] to your mind from the vicissitudes themselves.

You should accustom yourself to generating only the feeling of liking them. To do this, you should cease to view harmful circumstances as negative and should make every effort to train yourself to view them as valuable [*Yon-Tan*], because whether things are pleasing or not depends on how your mind perceives them. For example, if a person is continuously aware of the faults in worldly pursuits, then, if his retinue and wealth increase, he will feel all the more revulsion toward them. On the other hand, if a person perceives worldly pursuits as beneficial, he will even aspire [*Yid-sMon*] to increase his majestic power.

By practicing this kind of training, your mind will become gentle. Your attitude will become broad. You will become easy to be with. You will have a courageous mind. Your spiritual training will become free from obstacles. All bad circumstances will arise as glorious and auspicious. Your mind will always be satisfied by the joy [*bDe-Ba*] of peace.

To practice the path of enlightenment in this age of dregs, you must never be without the armor of this kind of training. When you are not afflicted by the suffering of anxiety, not only will other sufferings disappear, like weapons dropping from the hands of soldiers, but in most cases, even the real negative forces, such as illnesses themselves, will automatically disappear. The Holy Ones of the past said:

> By not feeling any dislike toward or discontent about anything, your mind will remain undisturbed. When your mind is not disturbed, your energy[11] will not be disturbed, and thereby other elements of the body will also not be disturbed. Because of this, your mind will not be disturbed, and so the wheel of joy will keep revolving.

They also said:

> As birds find it easy to injure horses and donkeys with sores on their backs, evil spirits or negative forces will easily find the opportunity to harm those whose nature is fearful. But it will be difficult to harm those whose nature is stable or strong.

Learned people realize that all happiness and suffering depend upon the mind and therefore seek happiness from the mind itself. They understand that, because the causes of happiness are complete [*Tshang*] within us, they are not dependent on external sources. With this realization, no matter what the afflictions, whether from beings or physical matter, they will not be able to hurt us. This same strength of mind shall also be with us at the time of death. We will always be free from the control of external afflictions.

The absorption (samādhi)[12] of Bodhisattvas known as "Overpowering of All Elements by Happiness" [*Ch'os Thams-Chad bDe-Bas Zil-Gyis Non-Pa*] is also accomplished by this means.

Instead of seeking happiness within their minds, foolish people chase after external objects, hoping thereby to find happiness. But the pursuit of any worldly happiness, whether great or small, presents those people seeking it with many failures, such as their not being able to attain it, to associate with it, or to keep it in balance. For such foolish people, as a proverb says, "Control is in the hands of others as if their hair were tangled in a tree."[13]

Enemies and robbers will find it easy to harm these foolish people. Even a little criticism will drive happiness away from their minds. Their happiness will never be reliable but will be as when a crow nurses a baby cuckoo: however much the crow nurtures the baby, it will be impossible for the baby cuckoo to become a baby crow. When such is the case, there will be nothing that is not tiresome for the gods [positive forces], miserable for demons [negative forces], and suffering for them [the foolish people].

This heart-advice is the condensation of a hundred different crucial points in one. There are many other instructions, such as how to accept the hardship of asceticism [*dKa'-sPyad*] for practicing the path, and how to turn illness and harmful effects into the path, as taught in Zhiche [*Zhi-Byed*] teachings and so on. But here I have just written an easily understandable outline on accepting suffering as the support based on the teachings of Śāntideva and his learned followers.

BY MEANS OF ABSOLUTE TRUTH [*Don-Dam*]

This is how to draw your mind to dwell contemplatively in supreme peace [*mCh'og-Tu Zhi-Ba*], the natural state of emptiness [*gNas-Lugs sTong-Pa*], in which unfavorable circumstances or even their names cannot be found, and how it is realized by means of reasoning-knowledge [*Rigs-Pa*] such as the "Refutation of the Arising of Phenomena from Any of the Four Extremes" [*mTha'-bZhi'i sKye-'Gog*].[14]

Even when you are out of that contemplative state, you should overcome unfavorable circumstances by seeing them as being hollow, mere names, and as not arising in the manner that feelings of suffering arose in your mind when fear and intimidation occurred in the past.

THE WAY OF TAKING HAPPINESS AS THE PATH TO ENLIGHTENMENT

BY MEANS OF RELATIVE TRUTH [*Kun-rDzob*]

If you slip under the control of happy circumstances or things that cause happiness, you will become proud, arrogant, and complacent, and this will obstruct your path toward enlightenment. But it is difficult not to fall under the sway of happiness, for, as Phadampa[15] says, "Men can bear great suffering, but only a little happiness."

Therefore consider how all the various phenomena of happiness and their sources are impermanent and full of suffering. Make efforts to develop a strong revulsion [*sKyo-Shas*] toward them and to turn your mind away from careless behavior.

Again, you ought to think, "All the wealth and happiness of the world are insigificant and are linked with much harm. Nevertheless, some of it has value, as the Buddha says:

> For a person whose freedom is impaired by suffering, it is very difficult to achieve enlightenment; but it will be easy for a person to achieve enlightenment if he is in comfort.

It is my great good fortune to have the opportunity to practice Dharma in happiness. Now I must buy Dharma with this happiness, and from the Dharma happiness will arise continuously. So I should train in making Dharma and happiness each other's support. Otherwise, like boiling water in a wooden pot, the final outcome will be the very same as what it was at the beginning."[16] Thus you should achieve the essential goal of life by uniting whatever happiness and joy arises with Dharma. This is the view of the *Ratnāvalī*.[17]

If you are happy but do not recognize [*Ngos Ma-Zin*] it, your happiness will not become the instrument of Dharma training and you will be wasting your life with the hope of a separate happiness. Therefore, as the antidote to the hopes for having a separate happiness, you should apply appropriate methods among the trainings given above and should possess the ambrosia of contentment [*Ch'og-Shes Kyi bDud-rTsi*].

There are other ways to take happiness as the path, such as those based on the "Instructions on Training in Bodhicitta" and on "Remembering the Kindness of the Three Precious Jewels." For the time being, however, this much is sufficient.

Further, in order to accept happiness as the path, as explained in the case of suffering, you should alternate the trainings of purification [*sByang*] with the accumulation of merit [*bSags*] in a solitary place.

BY MEANS OF ABSOLUTE TRUTH [*Don-Dam*]

You should understand it ("The Way of Accepting Happiness as the Path by Means of Absolute Truth") by the training given earlier (that is, the training on suffering.)[18]

CONCLUSION

If you cannot practice Dharma because of sorrow when you are suffering, and if you cannot practice Dharma because of your attachment to happiness when you are happy, then it will be impossible for you to have a chance to practice Dharma. So if you practice Dharma, there is nothing more essential than this training.

If you have this training, whatever kind of place you stay in, whether in a solitary place or a city; whatever the friends you associate with, whether good or bad; in whatever situation you find yourself, whether in riches or poverty, happiness or sorrow; whatever conversations you hear, whether praise or condemnation, good or bad, you will never be afraid [*Dogs-Pa'i 'Jigs-Pa*] that it might diminish you. Thus this training is called "the lionlike training."

Then whatever you do, your mind will be at ease and relaxed. Your attitude will be pure. Your final accomplishments will be excellent. Even though, physically, you are living in this impure land, your mind will be enjoying the glory of inconceivable bliss [peace] like the Bodhisattvas of the pure lands. As the Kadampa Lamas[19] say:

> By means of such training happiness will be brought under control and suffering will be ended. If you are alone, it will be the companion of sadness. If you are sick, it will nurse you.

Goldsmiths purify gold by melting it and make it flexible by rinsing it in water again and again. It is likewise with the mind: if, by taking happiness as the path, you develop ardent desire for the practice of the Dharma, and if, by taking suffering as the path, you cleanse your mind, then you shall easily attain the extraordinary absorption [samādhi] that makes your mind and body capable of accomplishing what you wish.

I can see that this training is the most profound method for perfecting moral discipline, the root of the virtues. Because it generates nonattachment to happiness, the foundation of the extraordinary moral discipline of renunciation [*Rab-Tu Byung-Ba*][20] is established. Because it generates freedom from the fear of suffering, it makes the discipline [*Tshul-Khrims*] pure. As it is said:

> Giving is the basis of moral discipline. Patience is the cleanser of moral discipline.

By training this way now, when you reach the higher stages of the path your attainments will come about as it is said:[21]

Bodhisattvas realize that all phenomena are like
Māyā,[22]
And they see that their births in saṃsāra are like
entering a joyful garden.[23]
Therefore, either at the time of prosperity or decline—
They will not experience the danger of either
emotional defilements or suffering.

Here are some illustrations from the life of the Buddha: Before attaining enlightenment, he renounced the universal rulership as if it were straw and sat by the Nairanjana River with no concern for the harshness of the austerities that he was practicing. This indicates that the development of equal taste [*Ro-sNyom*] of happiness and suffering was necessary for him to achieve the ambrosia (that is, full enlightenment).

After the Buddha attained enlightenment, on the one hand, the chiefs of human beings and gods up to the highest realms placed his feet on the crowns of their heads and offered him respect and service for all his needs and comfort. On the other hand, the Brahman Bharadvaja abused him with a hundred allegations, a Brahmin's daughter slandered him with accusations of sexual misconduct, and he lived on rotten horse fodder for three months in the country of King Agnidatta, and so forth. Yet throughout all these the Buddha remained without any alternations of mind, excitement, or depression, just like Mount Sumeru, which cannot be moved by the wind. This indicates that it is necessary to develop equal taste of happiness and suffering in order to act for the benefit of living beings.

Colophon

It is appropriate for this teaching to be taught by those who are like the Lord Kadampas, who have a history of "not crying when there is suffering" and of having "great revulsion toward saṃsāra when there is happiness." If a man like me teaches it, I am afraid that my own tongue will have contempt for me. But with my goal of achieving the habit of "equal taste" of the eight worldly affairs [*Ch'os-brGyad*], I, the poor old man Tenpe Nyima, have written this in the Forest of Many Birds.

8

Entering into the Path of Enlightenment Taking Daily Activities as the Path, According to the Unified Approach of Sūtra and Tantra

Rigdzin Jigme Lingpa

Homage to the Omniscient One! A person who earnestly wishes to attain the state of liberation should accumulate merit and wisdom and purify defilements through various means. Since the Omniscient One [the Buddha] has great skill-in-means and compassion, he has expounded methods for amassing inconceivable good as just an automatic consequence of performing daily activities. Here I am condensing and expounding them for the benefit of those with average intelligence.

First, in the morning when you are wide awake, develop your intention, thinking: "May all sentient beings awaken from ignorance!"

When you get out of bed, think: "May all sentient beings achieve the Body of Buddha!"

As you dress, think: "May all sentient beings wear the clothing of self-respect and decorum!"

While fastening your belt, think: "May all sentient beings be tied to the root of goodness!"

When you sit down, think: "May all sentient beings attain the Vajra Seat!"[1]

When you enter a house, think: "May all sentient beings enter the City [or state] of Liberation!"

When you sleep, think: "May all sentient beings attain the Dharmakāya of the Buddhas!"

When you dream, think: "May all sentient beings recognize all phenomena as unreal, like dreams!"

At the time of preparing food, when the flame rises up, develop the certainty that this very flame has always been identical in nature to the White-Robed Consort.[2] Then visualize the form of the syllable HŪṂ in the midst of the fire and transform it into the Fire Vajra Ḍākinī.[3] Her body is black, she has one head and two hands, holding vajra and bell with the hūṃkāra mudrā, her right leg is folded and her left leg advanced, and she is adorned with various jewel-ornaments. Her mouth is open, and her tongue is marked with the syllable RAṂ. Her tongue is the embodiment of the tongues of all the Buddhas of the three times. Place some mustard seeds in front of you, and visualize that your unvirtuous karma and defilements are dwelling in your own heart in the form of the black syllable PAṂ, and that all this unvirtuous karma and defilement, amassed through the three doors of body, speech, and mind, has gathered in this syllable. Visualize the syllable RAṂ at your navel and the syllable YAṂ on the soles of your feet. From the visualized vital energy maṇḍala, spontaneously generated from the syllable YAṂ, the vital energy moves upward within the body and makes the flame, spontaneously generated from the syllable RAṂ, burn at your navel. The flame burns upward, causing the syllable PAṂ to spring out of your nostrils, like a deer chased out by a hunter. It then dissolves, as the form of a horned scorpion, into the mustard seeds. Repeating "OṂ ĀḤ HŪṂ" many times, mentally transform the nature of these mustard seeds into that nectar. Then while reciting:

> OṂ VAJRAḌĀKA KHA KHA KHĀHI KHĀHI SARVA PĀPAṂ DAHANA BHASMĪKURUYE SVĀHĀ
> [OM BADZAR DAKA KHAKHA KHAHI KHAHI SARVAPAPAM DAHANABHASMI KURUYE SOHA],[4]

offer the mustard seeds into the stove with the thumb and the forefinger. When the material substance is consumed, confess the mistakes made in doing this practice by reciting the Hundred-Syllable Mantra[5] of Vajrasattva three times. Then, upon your saying "VAJRA MU," imagine that the Wisdom Deity returns to its own abode in the Pure Land, and that the Visualized Deity becomes inseparably mixed with the fire. Then dedicate the merits of this practice to all sentient beings.

While walking, you should think that you are circumambulating the Buddha Pure Lands, as many as there are atoms in the universe.

When you happen to put on new clothes, you should purify them into the state of emptiness by reciting the Svabhāva mantra.[6] Then visualize that from the state of emptiness, from the syllable TRĀṂ, priceless celestial clothing emerges. Then mentally make offerings to the direction in which your Root-Lama is dwelling. Thereafter visualize yourself in the form of your tutelary deity, whoever it is, and put on your clothes.

When you bathe and go into water, since the water has always been identical in nature to Māmakī,[7] you should become convinced of this. Visualize the water in the form of the syllable BAṂ, from which the Water Vajra Ḍākinī emerges, then recite:

> VAJRA-ḌĀKKI ŚĀNTIṂ-KURU SVĀHĀ
> [BADZAR DAKI SHANTING KURU SOHA]

and pray for the pacification of illness, evil forces, and defilements. Finally, imagine the Ḍākinī melting into light and then becoming nectar. Then washe or bathe.

When eating lunch or any meal, arrange the food in front of you. To take the objects of enjoyment as the Path is a special attribute of Tantra. But until one can actualize the power of the stages of development and perfection, or at least obtain the warmth of a meditative experience, one should not commit any actions that may deflect one into states in which there can be no accumulation of merit nor any states in which there can be any wrongdoing—thereby indicating that the necessity of proper conduct has been neglected in favor of proper view. Nor should you have attachment to rigid conduct, by which proper view is neglected in favor of proper conduct. This is the exceptional view of the Second Buddha of Orgyen [Padmasambhava]. Therefore, if one has meat, or alcohol, and so on, to consume, one should understand as follows: in the words of the Buddha it is said, "I do not and I shall not permit meat as food to anyone," and it is said, "From now on it is not permitted for my Śrāvakras to eat meat." Thus he announced the rules. You should think about this, thus: "Well, in the situation of those who follow Vajrayāna, if they have attained the power of contemplation, they will not be affected by obscurations. And if one is capable of benefiting sentient beings by the connection established by enjoying their meat, it is well done. But I do not have such confidence, for there has been no sentient being who has not been my parent. It is certain that the owner of the meat [that is, the animal] must have been my parent in previous lives, as in the story about Ārya Katyāyana wandering for alms.[8] If so, if a butcher kills my present parents and serves their meat to me, can I desire to eat it? Ah, how pitiful!"

When you think thus, if you're normal-minded, there is no alternative but for your heart to shrink, and for you irresistibly to develop compassion toward the animal. At that point, even if you can't develop perfect Bodhicitta, it is certain that you will develop an attitude close to it. Without diminishing the force of that compassionate thought, you should recite such mantras as the *Kaṃkani*,[9] the *Uṣṇīṣa dhāraṇī*,[10] and the heart mantra of Tag-Trol[11] [liberation by wearing, *bTags Grol*], as many as you can, and blow on the meat. Make strong prayers of aspiration for the animal. This is called "emptiness functioning as karmic cause and result." If one cannot understand this, and yet claims to be a tantric practitioner, enjoying meat and alcohol carefreely, then how would there be a difference between such a person and a sparrow, hawk, or wolf?

In the same way, also for alcohol, even if you use it as a sacred [*Dam-Tshig*] substance of the Vajrayāna, if you drink it like a lay person without blessing it by saying: "OṂ ĀḤ HŪṂ HA HO HRĪḤ," it is said that you will destroy both your sacred vow and attainments. In *Saṃvarodaya* [*sDom-'Byung*], it is said:

> Without reciting three "HA," and so forth
> If a sacred vow-holder drinks
> It will become poisonous, of this there is no doubt.
> No accomplishments of Tantra will be achieved.

Also, concerning the quantity, you should not drink more than a full skull-cup. If you drink more than that and become intoxicated, then you will be reborn in the hell of "Crying for Help." In a Tantra it is said:

> For whomever becomes intoxicated by alcohol
> Many obstructions will occur.
> A tantrika who becomes drunk on alcohol
> Will be tortured in the realm of "Crying for Help."

Now you may think: "Did not Ācārya Padmasambhava and Siddha Virūpa and others consume five hundred kegs of alcohol at one time?" But it is said in histories that, for them, not only was there no question of becoming intoxicated by drinking five hundred kegs of alcohol, but they were not even sated; and that they stopped the sun from setting when they could not pay the tavern bill.

Now if you can act similarly, consuming undiluted poison, imprisoning the sun and moon, moving mountains here and there, and flying in the sky, then it will be of benefit for the Teaching in general, and in particular for the Vajrayāna, for you will be able to transform phenomena to help those of reversed faith [that is, for those who have lost true faith]. There will be reason for great gratitude to you! Otherwise, if your perceptions become instantly deluded due to alcohol, so that you act like a madman whose vital energy has entered the heart-vein, speaking and behaving unpredictably—well, if such behavior, however improbable, is really due to your spiritual attainment, then of course that is wonderful! But remember, in a scripture it is said:

> In the age of darkness
> They will quote tantric sources that say
> That the sacred substances of meat and alcohol are proper to use.
> Without the warmth of meditative experience
> Everyone will be introduced to meat, blood, and alcohol.
> They will thereby slyly show contempt for those who do practice according to the Dharma,

Saying that these practitioners have taken no sacred
vows.
People like that will come at the final period of the
Teaching.
Alas, alas, except for hell
There is no place for them to go. How pitiful!

Therefore, you should be certain about what to accept and reject. You should partake of food so as not to abuse the body, the basis of practice toward Enlightenment, regarding the food as a great assemblage of offering of sacred substances of the Vajrayāna to the various deities in the maṇḍala of the body. You should not partake of food simply for the purpose of being healthy and glowing. Recalling the three maṇḍalas[12] of the body, recite:

HO! The materials of food and drink are perfectly
pure,
Primordially being the great Assemblage of Offering.
By OṂ ĀḤ HŪṂ and HA HO HRĪḤ they are
Transformed into the nectar of great bliss and purity.
The aggregates, elements, and sense-fields of my body
Are the nature of those occupying the Complete Three
Seats[13]
And the deities of the Maṇḍala of the One Hundred
Glorious Buddha Families.[14]
In the state in which all movement is great bliss,
Which is the highest sacred Vajra obligation and
The great cloud of Enlightened Mind,
I enjoy the food in the state of nondual equanimity.
May I perfect the accumulations of the yogic path
Without the occurrence of any obscurations caused by
food,
And may the unstinting patron who gave this food also
Experience the fruits of the Mahāyāna!

Having recited this, you should then become certain, in this way, about recalling the purity of the Vajra Body: the soles of the feet are the maṇḍala of air; the place of the triple convergence is the maṇḍala of fire; the stomach is the maṇḍala of water; the heart is the maṇḍala of earth; the spine is Mount Meru; the head is the peak of Mount Meru. The maṇḍala of the body is equally dimensioned, so it is a square [the foundation of the maṇḍala palace]. The eight types of bone [*rKang*—two bones for each arm and leg] are the eight pillars of the maṇḍala palace. The eyes are the five rings of walls. The nose is the fringe and the teeth are the latticework hangings of the palace sides. The tongue and lips are the ramparts, and the ears are the pediments of the palace. The four veins, through which move the vital energy of the heart, are the four entrances to the palace. Primary consciousness is the Heruka[15] within the palace. The eight consciousnesses are the eight Gaurī [deities], and so on.[16] The eight objective fields are the eight Thra-Men-Ma[17] [*Phra-Men-Ma*]. The four extreme concepts are the four Door-protectors.[18] The twenty-eight vertebrae are the twenty-eight Lords.[19] The ten unvirtuous actions are the ten Wrathful Male Deities.[20] The ten virtuous actions are the ten Wrathful Female Deities.[21] The eighteen ribs are the eighteen Great Deputies.[22] The three hundred and sixty bones are the three hundred and sixty Messengers.[23] The seven doors of the faculties are the seven Ma-mo.[24] The twelve joints are the twelve Ten-ma [*bsTan-Ma*].[25]

In short, the body is primordially and spontaneously the nature of the five maṇḍalas; the body is the maṇḍala of channels; the channels are the maṇḍala of letters; the semen is the maṇḍala of nectar; the vital energy is the maṇḍala of wisdom; and intrinsic awareness [*Rig-Pa*] is the maṇḍala of Enlightenment.

Knowing the five fingers as the Goddesses of the five objects of enjoyment,[26] you should enjoy food and drink according to the sacred obligations of the four empowerments.[27] If you are a practitioner of the Path of Skillful Means [*Thabs-Lam*], you should enjoy food and so on as an offering, perceiving it as the nectar of bliss and emptiness, without wavering in this awareness even for a moment. If you are a practitioner of the Path of Liberation [*Grol-Lam*], you should enjoy food and so on as an offering, perceiving it as uncontaminated nectar without wavering in this awareness. Your understanding of emptiness should be clear and pervading, so that no thought of bitter or sweet arises. This kind of knowledge should apply to all food and drink.

If you are not capable of that kind of understanding, or even if you can understand, but are an upholder of the divisions of the Buddhist Canon [*sDe-sNod 'Dzin-Pa*], that is, if you observe the Vinaya rules, and would like to make an offering of the first portion of your food before the midday meal, then you should do the following:

Bless the food as nectar by reciting OṂ ĀḤ HŪṂ. Then arrange the first portion of the food as an offering, and offer it to the Lama, saying:

> GURU VAJRA NAIVEDYE ĀḤ HŪṂ
> [GURU BADZAR NEVITYE AH HUNG].

Then offer it to the Three Jewels [the Buddha, Dharma and Saṅgha], saying:

> RATNA VAJRA NAIVEDYE ĀḤ HŪṂ
> [RATNA BADZAR NEVITYE AH HUNG].

Then offer it to the Great Compassionate One [Avalokiteśvara], saying:

> LOKEŚVARA VAJRA NAIVEDYE ĀḤ HŪṂ
> [LOKESHVARA BADZAR NEVITYE AH HUNG].

Make offering to the Three Roots [Guru, Deva, Ḍākinī], saying:

> OṂ ĀḤ HŪṂ GURU DEVA ḌĀKINĪ VAJRA NAIVEDYE ĀḤ HŪṂ
> [OM AH HUNG GURU DEVA DAKINI BADZAR NEVITYE AH HUNG].

Then offer a handful ('Ch'ang-Bu) to Hārītī[28] [*'Phrog-Ma*], saying:

> OṂ HĀRĪTE PAṆḌA AKHAṂ SVĀHĀ
> [OM HARITI PANTI AKHAM SOHA].

Now offer a handful to the five hundred sons of Hārītī, saying:

> OṂ HĀRĪTE PAṆṬINI KHAṂ SVĀHĀ
> [OM HARITI PANTINI KHAM SOHA].

Give a handful to the elements or spirits, which have a right to the first portion of food, saying:

> OṂ AGRAPAṆḌA-AŚIBHYAḤ SVĀHĀ
> [OM ATRAPANI ASHIBHYE SOHA].

Then enjoy the food by yourself, practicing the yoga of eating. Or, if you cannot, then enjoy the food with compassion for the bacteria [*Srin-'Bu*] living in the body, with the intention to serve them with food for now, and finally, when you have attained Enlightenment, to serve them with Dharma.

After eating, give one handful to the elements or spirits that have the right to the remainder, saying:

> OṂ UCCHAṢṬA-PAṆḌA-AŚIBHYAḤ SVĀHĀ
> [OM UTSITRA PANTA ASHIBHYE SOHA].

Then wash your mouth.

Then recite the dhāraṇī for the fulfillment of obligations incurred from the offerings of food preceded by the following prayer:

> CHOM-DEN-DE DE-ZHIN SHEG-PA DRA-CHOM-PA YANG-DAG-PAR DZOG-PE SANG-GYE KUN-NE OD-KYI GYAL-PO ME-OD RAB-TU SAL-WA LA CHAG-TSHAL-LO.

[I pay homage to the Clear Blazing Flame, the Lord of Total Light, the Fully Enlightened One, Subduer of all the Foes and Thus Gone One.]

> NAMAḤ SAMANTA-PRABHĀ-RĀJĀYA TATHĀGATĀYA ARHATE SAMYAKSAṂBUDDHĀYA TAD YATHĀ NAMO MAÑJUŚRĪYE KUMĀRA BHŪTĀYA BODHISATTVĀYA MAHĀSATTVĀYA MAHĀKARUṆIKĀYA TAD YATHĀ OṂ NIRĀLAMBNE NIRĀBHĀSE JAYA JAYA LABHE MAHĀMATE DAKṢE DAKṢIṆI PARIŚODHĀYA SVĀHĀ

> [NAMA SAMANTA PRABHA RAJAYA TATHAGATAYA ARHATE SAMYAKSAM-BUDDHAYA TADYATHA NAMO MANJUSHRIYE KUMARA BHUTAYA BODHISATOYA MAHASATOYA MAHAKARUNIKAYA TADYATHA OM NIRALAMBE NIRABHASE DZAYE DZAYA LABADHE MAHAMATE DAKSHEDAKSHENAM PARISHODHAYA SOHA]

The one who gives, the one to whom alms are given
And that which is given—not conceptualizing these
By the power of that equanimity in giving,
May the patron attain full perfection!

Recite one hundred times the mantra given in the *Mañjuśrī-mūla-tantra* for dispelling the harmful effects of eating meat:

OṂ ĀḤ VĪRA HŪṂ ŚECARA MAṂ
[OM AH BHIRA HUNG KHETSARA MAM].

and blow upon the bones. Then say the prayer of aspiration:

May the animal not experience the sufferings of the
three lower realms
And without any hardship
May it achieve birth in a body more extraordinary than
the gods
And thereafter swiftly attain Buddhahood!

On occasions of disposing of impurities, you should give away the bodily impurities as stated in the *Acalakalpa-tantra.*

For spittle:

OṂ ĀḤ SU AHARIBHYA SVĀYĀ
[OM ASHU AHARI BHYE SOHA].

For mucus:

OṂ SIṄGANA AHARIBHYA SVĀHĀ
[OM SINGANA AHARI BHYE SOHA].

For bodily impurities in general:

OṂ MALA AHARIBHYA SVĀHĀ
[OM MALA AHARI BHYE SOHA].

For feces:

OṂ BHITA AHARIBHYA SVĀHĀ
[OM BHITA AHARI BHYE SOHA].

For urine:

OḤ NUÑCA AHARIBHYA SVĀHĀ
[OM NUNTSA AHARI BHYE SOHA].

For general remains:

> OṂ UCCHIṢṬA AHARIBHYA SVĀHĀ
> [OM UTSTSHITA AHARI BHYE SOHA].

By reciting thus on the various occasions, there will automatically result great alms for the hungry spirits [*Yi-Dags*].

Some special mantras for multiplying the effect of practices are as follows: If you recite the following mantra while circumambulating stūpas, and so on, one circumambulation becomes in effect ten million:

> NAMO BHAGAVATE RATNAKETURĀJĀYA TATHĀGATĀYA ARHATE SAMYAKSAMBUDDHĀYA TAD YATHĀ OṂ RATNE RATNE MAHĀRATNE RATNAVIJAYE SVĀHĀ
> [NAMO BHAGAVATE RATNAKETURADZAYA TATHAGATAYA ARHATE SAMYAKSAM-BUDDHAYA TADYATHA OM RATNE RATNE MAHARATNE RATNA BHIDZAYA SOHA].

If you must tread on shadows of stūpas and so on, due to the position of the sun or moon, go into the shadow imagining that you are lifting it up and recite:

> VAJRA VEGĀKRAMA HŪṂ
> [BADZAR VEGA TRAMA HUNG]

and this will dispel the ill effects. When you pay homage, including prostrations, recite:

> OṂ NAMO MAÑJUŚRĪYE NAMO SUŚRIYE NAMO UTTAMAŚRIYE SVĀHĀ
> [OM NAMO MANJUSHRIYE NAMO SUSHRIYE NAMO UTTAMASHRIYE SOHA].

The multiplication in effect will be as above (that is, by a factor of ten million). Similarly, when you make offerings of flowers, if you offer the flower while reciting the following mantra seven times, each flower will become in effect one million flowers:

> OṂ NAMO BHAGAVATE PUṢPAKETURĀJĀYA TATHĀGATĀYA ARHATE SAMYAKSAMBUDDHĀYA TAD YATHĀ OṂ PUṢPE PUṢPE MAHĀPUṢPA SUPUṢPA-UDBHAVE PUṢPASAMBHAVE PUṢPAAVAKĪRAṆE SVĀHĀ

[OM NAMO BHAGAVATE PUPE KETURADZAYA TATHAGATAYA ARHATE SAMYAKSAM-BUDDHAYA TADYATHA OM PUPE PUPE MAHAPUPEPUPE SUPUPE URBHAVEPUPE SAMBHAVEPUPE AVAKERANI SOHA].

If a person must use the offerings, such as the keeper of a temple, by reciting the following mantra it is said that he will not incur ill effects and that the offerings will become empowered substances [*dNgos-Grub*]:

OṂ DEVĀYA NĀMA NIDHASA SVĀHĀ
[OM DEVAYA NAMA NIDHASA SOHA].

Recitations for the multiplication of general virtuous practices are as follows:

OṂ SAMBHARA SAMBHARA VIMANASARA MAHĀ JAMBHA HŪṂ PHAṬ
[OM SAMBHARA SAMBHARA VIMANASARA MAHADZAMBHA HUNG PHAT]

and:

OṂ RUCIRA MAṆI PRAVARTĀYA SVĀHĀ
[OM RITSIRA MANI PRAVARTAYA SOHA].

CONCLUSION

In all of these recitations it is important to develop an attitude devoid of conceptions regarding everything, and then afterward to perform dedication of the merit accrued and aspirations for the welfare of all beings. This simple explanation was composed by Dzogchenpa Rangchung Dorje (i.e., Kunkhyen Jigme Lingpa).

[What follows is the Tibetan manuscript of *mDo-sNgags Zung-Du 'Jug-Pa'i sPyod-Yul Lam-Khyer Sangs-rGyas Lam-Zhugs Zhes-Bya-Ba,* which appears above in translation as *Entering into the Path of Enlightenment: Taking Daily Activities as the Path, According to the Unified Approach of Sūtra and Tantra.* The manuscript was handwritten by the author, Rigdzin Jigme Lingpa, but the last folio of the original has been lost. The missing folio was added by Kyala Khenpo (1892–1936) of Dodrup Chen monastery in Golok, eastern Tibet. Part of the personal collection of Khenpo Kome of Dodrup Chen monastery, the manuscript is now in the possession of Tulku Thondup.]

1a

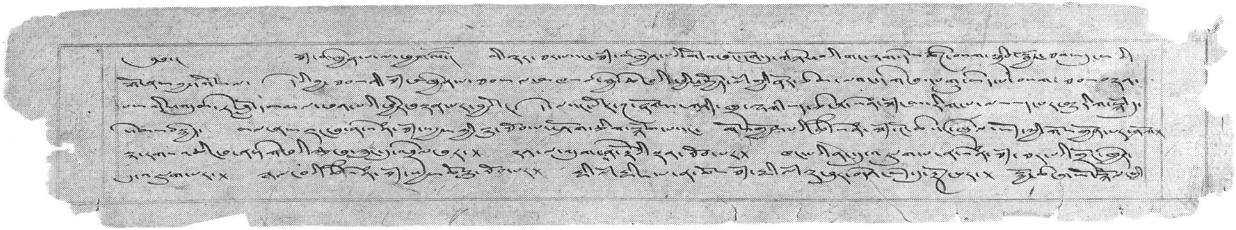

1b

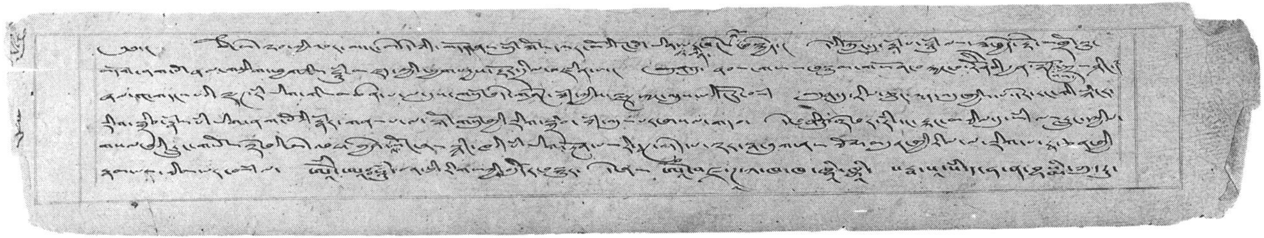

2a

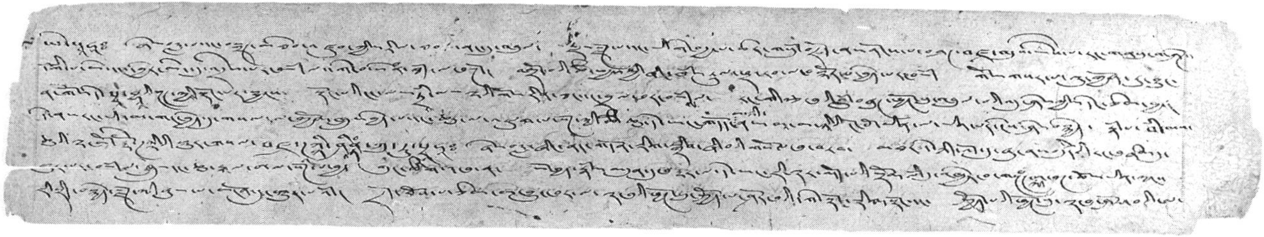

2b

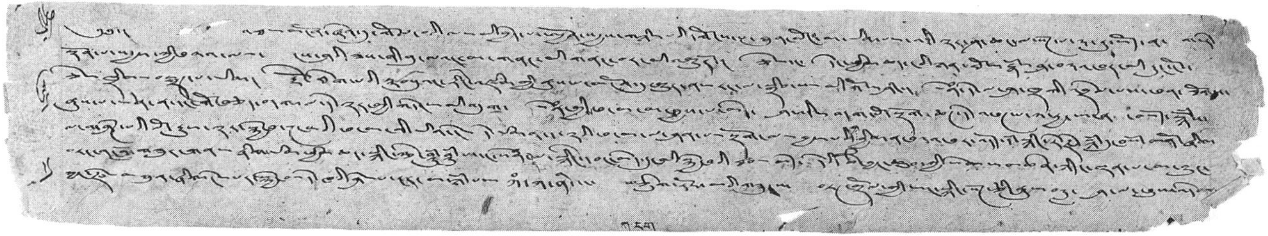

3a

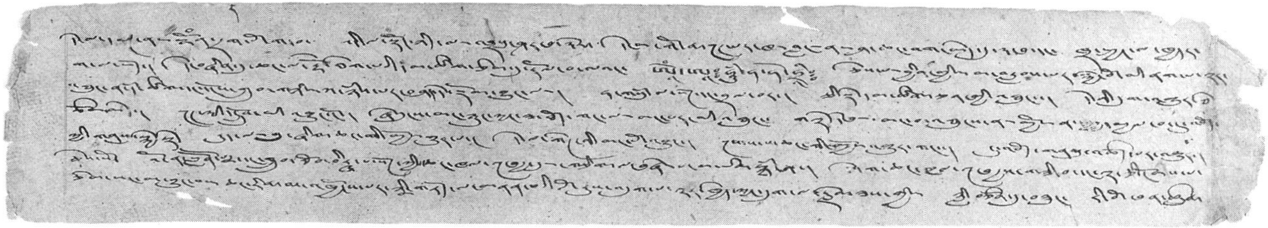

3b

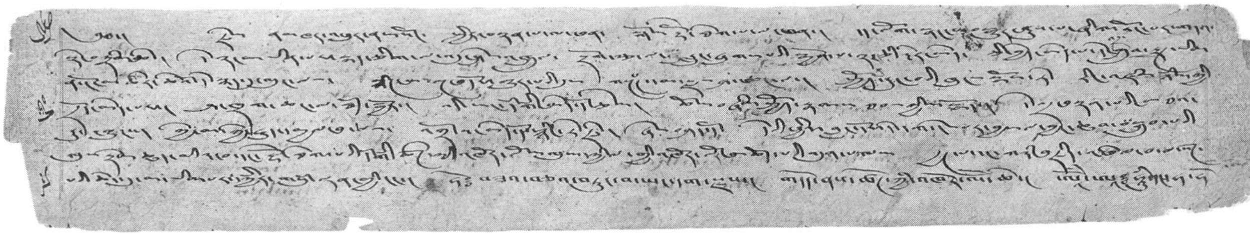

4a

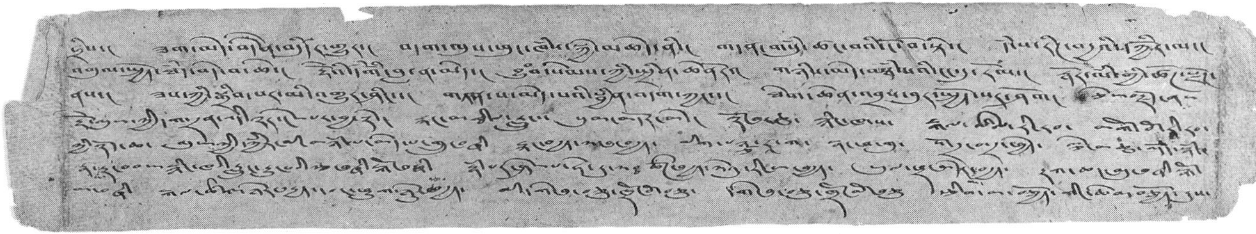

4b

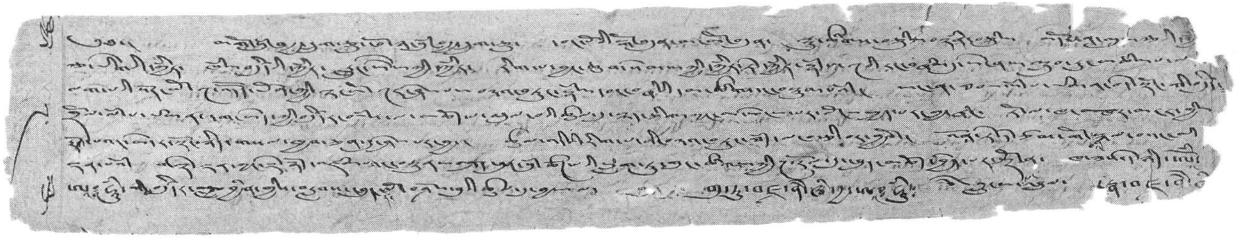

5a

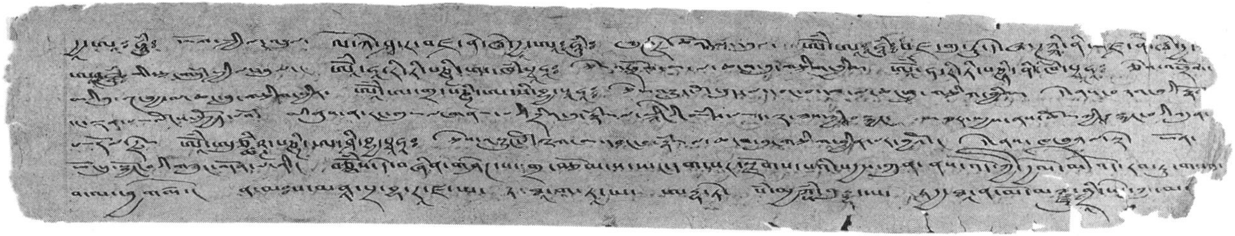

5b

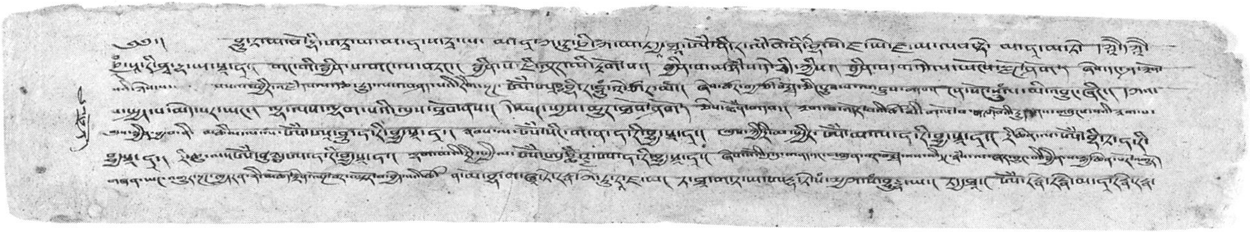

6a

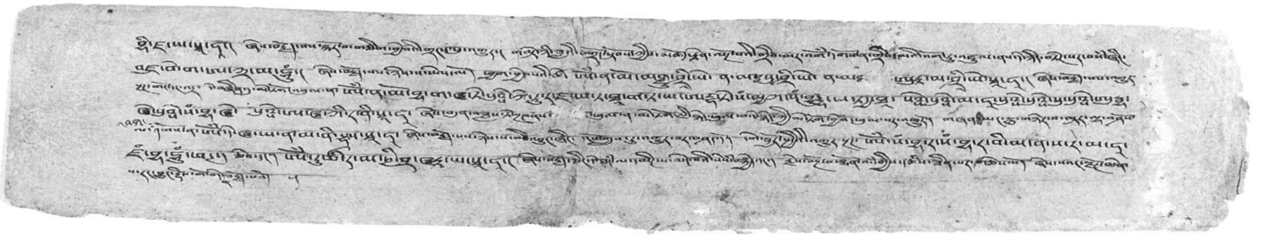

6b

Key to Abbreviations of Works Cited

BP — Byang-Ch'ub Sems-dPa'i sPyod-Pa-La 'Jug-Pa by Śāntideva. Dodrup Chen monastery edition.

DC — Srid-Pa Ma-Mo sGang-Shar Gyi Phrin-Las Khrigs-bsDebs rNam-gSal-Du bKod-Pa bDe-Ch'en Ch'ar-'Bebs (discovered by Ra-Shag) by 'Ch'i-Med bsTan-gNyis Gling-Pa [Kong-sPrul] from Rinchen Terdzod, Vol. Khi. Palpung edition, reproduced by Jamyang Khyentse.

DP — Dharmapada, canonical scripture.

DR — Srid-Pa Ma-Mo sGang-Shar Gyi dKyil-'Khor Ch'en-Por dBang-bKur Ba'i Ch'o-Ga gSal-Bar bKod-Pa bDe-Ch'en Rol-mTsho by Padma Blo-Gros mTha'-Yas-Pa'i sDe [Kong-sPrul], Rinchen Terdzod, Vol. Khi. Palpung edition, reproduced by Jamyang Khyentse.

DT — Srid-Pa Ma-Mo sGang-Shar Gyi Phrin-Las sNying-Por Dril-Ba bDe-Ch'en Thig-Le (discovered by Ra-Shag) by Padma Gar-dBang Phrin-Las 'Gro-'Dul-rTsal [Kong-sPrul?], Rinchen Terdzod, Vol. Khi. Palpung edition, reproduced by Jamyang Khyentse.

GDN — Klong-Ch'en sNying-Gi Thig-Le'i mKha'-'Gro bDe-Ch'en rGyal-Mo'i bsGrub-gZhung Gi 'Grel-Ba rGyud-Don sNang-Ba (or Ratik) by Ngag-dBang bsTan-'Dzin rDo-rJe. Gra-Nang rGyal-Tshogs sKyed-Tshal edition, reproduced by Sonam T. Kazi.

KLZ — Kun-bZang Bla-Ma'i Zhai-Lung by O-rGyan 'Jigs-Med Ch'os-Kyi dBang-Po [Paltrul Rinpoche]. Rumtek edition.

NGJ — bChom-lDan-'Das rDo-rJe Phur-Ba rGyud-Lugs Las dBang-Ch'og dNgos-Grub rGya-mTsho'i 'Jug-Ngog by Jigme Lingpa. Dege edition reproduced by Dodrup Chen Rinpoche.

PCM dPal gSang-Ba'i sNying-Po De Kho-Na-Nyid Nges-Pa'i rGyud-Kyi 'Grel-Pa Phyogs-bChu'i Mun-Pa Thams-Chad rNam-Par Sel-Ba by rDo-rJe gZi-brJid [Longchen Rabjam]. Published by Darthang Tulku Kun-ga.

SB sNyigs-Dus 'Gro-Ba Yongs-Kyi sKyabs-mGon Zhabs-dKar rDo-rJe-'Ch'ang Ch'en-Po'i rNam-Par-Thar-Pa rGyas-Par bShad-Pa sKal-bZang gDul-Bya Thar-'Dod rNams-Kyi Re-Ba bsKong-Ba'i Yid-bZhin Nor-Bu bSam-'Phel dBang-rGyal, [Autobiography of Zhabs-dKar Tshogs-Drug Rang-Grol]. bKra-Shis 'Khyil edition, reproduced by Jamyang Khyentse.

SN rDzogs-Pa Ch'en-Po Sems-Nyid Ngal-gSo by Dri-Med A'od-Zer [Longchen Rabjam]. Adzom edition, reproduced by Dodrup Chen Rinpoche.

UD Upadeśa. A collection of writings by Longchen Rabjam, Paltrul, and Mipham.

Notes

Introduction

1. Fully Awakened One or Fully Enlightened One. *Buddha* refers to the principle of enlightenment and to any enlightened individual, such as Śākyamuni, the historical Buddha. Here it refers to the historical Buddha.
2. An ardent Mahāyāna trainee who has taken the Bodhicitta vow (see n. 1 to chapter 1). These include beginners as well as highly enlightened ones; when they become fully enlightened they are known as Buddhas.
3. The Buddhist teachings, which consist of the scriptures and the spiritual training with its different levels of attainments.
4. In contrast to enlightenment, saṃsāra is the vicious cycle of existence, the mundane world. It arises out of ignorance, functions through the cause and effect of emotional actions, and is characterized by suffering.
5. See Tshega's *Sheche Zegma (Shes-Bya'i Zegs-Ma),* n. 35 (Beijing: Mirig Petrun Khang).
6. Tib.: *gChod.* The tantric ritual and meditational practice for overcoming the four demons (negative energies): the demons of the body, death, pleasure, and emotional defilements.
7. (1) Buddha, the enlightened guide who shows the path of enlightenment,
   (2) Dharma, the path of enlightenment with its attainments, and
   (3) Saṅgha, the community that pursues the path of enlightenment.

1. *The Heart Essence*

1. The Awakened Mind (Bodhicitta). This is a mind aspiring to serve all living beings without self-interest and to pursue training in the six perfections.
2. This reference to Chogyal Thrisong Deutsan should probably be to King Songtsen Gampo, because he is the king who proclaimed the Sixteen Principles of Pure Human Conduct.

2. *Holy Dharma Advice*

1. The law of the cause and effect of actions—that every action one performs has a commensurate effect in this and future lives.
2. A form of vocative exclamation.
3. A vocative exclamation.
4. A type of evil spirit.
5. Another type of evil spirit.
6. A joyous exclamation.
7. Tib.: *sNyigs-Ma.* This age has five characteristics indicating degeneration: short life span, emotional struggles, perverted views, sentient beings difficult to tame, and declining prosperity.
8. These are eight kinds of worldly attitudes. They are: wanting to have gain, fame, praise, and happiness, and wanting not to have loss, infamy, blame, or suffering.
9. He is the embodiment of the compassion of the Buddhas who manifests in the form of a Bodhisattva.

6. *A Letter of Spiritual Advice*

1. The word *chal* is onomatopœia for a splash. In the story of chal, a fox was frightened by the "chal" sound made by a tree branch falling into a pond. As he ran away, each species of animal that questioned the fox communicated the fear to the next species, and they all believed that there was a big dangerous animal called a "chal" chasing them. Finally a lion took them back to the pond to investigate and they learned the truth. This is an allegory about listening to peoples' notions and claims and acting upon them instead of investigating the truth for oneself.

7. *Instructions on Turning Happiness and Suffering into the Path of Enlightenment*

1. The following verse is from the *Śiṣyalekha* by Chandragomin. Page 46b/5, Vol. Nge, sPring Yig, Tenjur, Dege edition.
2. An alternate translation of this line is:

   He remains free from the experiences of happiness and suffering.
3. Tib.: *bZe-Re.* This is a key word in the text. "Being susceptible or overly sensitive" could be closer to the meaning. Also, "impatience," "paranoia," or "panic."

4. If we view an object as unfavorable and suffer because of it, it will disturb our normal state of mind. So when such an attitude arises, instead of being overwhelmed by it, we should keep our mind in its own normal, relaxed state, without the attitude of dislike for the object and suffering because of it. Then our mind will be free from the control of others.
5. Of the six realms of saṃsāra constituting cyclic existence, three are designated "happy realms," namely the dwelling places of gods, demigods, and human beings. The remaining three are the "lower realms," inhabited by animals, hungry ghosts, and the beings in hell. Among them human beings have the easiest access to the possibility of enlightenment. They are the most capable of dealing with suffering and happiness in a spiritually creative way, which is the subject of this instruction.
6. The forces are: (1) to rely on a blessed support, (2) to generate sincere regret for evil deeds previously committed, (3) to pledge to refrain from committing evil deeds again, and (4) to apply antidotes that are the means of purification through spiritual training.
7. Tib.: *bsDam-Pa.* Literally, to seal, close, refrain, prevent, or bind.
8. Tib.: *dMigs-Pa.* Concentration, concept, or attitude.
9. An Indian sweetmeat, the taste of which is both sweet and spicy. Although it is hot, if you are used to it, it is enjoyable.
10. Tib.: *gYeng-Ba.* Literally, wandering, straying, or drifting.
11. Tib.: *rLung.* Inner energy or air.
12. This is the absorption in contemplative meditation. There are many kinds of levels of samādhis that bring tranquillity and peace to the mind.
13. Literally, "hair is in the hands of a tree." If your hair is caught in a tree you won't be free to move.
14. The four extremes: is, is not, both is and is not, and neither is nor is not.
15. An Indian saint who founded the Zhichedpa order in Tibet (11th century C.E.). His principal student was the Tibetan woman saint Machig Labdrön (*Ma-Chig Lab-sGron*), who propagated the Chö (*gChod*) teachings.
16. If you boil water in a wooden pot, the fire will burn it up. Similarly, if you do not know how to use happiness and Dharma practice as the support of each other, the happiness will be quickly exhausted and you will find yourself back at square one, seeking new happiness again.

17. By Nāgārjuna. Tibetan title: *Rin-Ch'en Phreng-Ba.*
18. That is, acceptance of suffering as the path.
19. Tib.: *bKa'-gDams.* This is the name of a school founded by the Indian scholar Atīśa in Tibet in the 11th century C.E.
20. Tib.: *Rab-Tu Byung.* Renunciation of household life.
21. *Mahāyāna-sutrālaṃḳāra-nāma-ḳāriḳā* by Maitreyanātha. Vol. Phi, Sems Tsam, Tenjur, Dege edition.
22. This line is on wisdom, which is the aspect of ultimate truth in Buddhism.
23. This line is on compassion, which is one of the aspects of skillful means in Buddhism.

8. *Entering the Path of Enlightenment*

1. *rDo-rJe'i sTan*: In the path it is the seat of unwavering contemplation, and in the result it is the state of changeless Buddhahood.
2. *Gos dKar-Mo* (S. Paṇḍaravāsinī): The White-Robed female deity is the deity of fire. There are five female deities, who correspond to the five elements. According to the path they are the means of transforming or purifying the five elements into the Buddha qualities, and according to the result they are the Buddha qualities themselves. Other female deities are: *Nam-mKha' dByings-Kyi dBang-Phyug-Ma* (S. Ākaśa-dhātvīśvari) for space, *Sangs-rGyas sPyan-Ma* (S. Locanā) for water, Māmakī for earth, and *Dam-Tshigs sGrol-Ma* (S. Samayatārā) for air.
3. *rDo-rJe mKha'-'Gro* (S. Vajra Ḍākinī): In the nature and form of this particular female deity described in the text one visualizes and sees the fire of the fire offering as the Vajra Ḍākinī.
4. Hereafter, all the mantras and dhāraṇīs which are in brackets are the Tibetanized pronunciation of the Sanskrit mantras and dhāraṇīs.
5. This mantra or dhāraṇī is for purification of the ill effects of the evil deeds and emotional traces. It is the seed syllables of the hundred "Peaceful and Wrathful" deities of the Vajrasattva maṇḍala.

In Sanskrit:

OṂ VAJRASATTVASAMAYAM ANUPĀLAYA VAJRASATTVA TVENOPATIṢṬHA ḌṚḌHO ME BHAVA SUTOṢYO ME BHAVA SUPOṢYO ME BHAVA ANURAKTO ME BHAVA SARVASIDDHIṂ ME PRAYACCHA SARVAKARMASU CA ME CITTAṂ ŚREYAḤ KURU HŪṂ HA HA HA HA HOḤ BHAGAVAN SARVATATHĀGATAVAJRA MĀ ME MUÑCA VAJRĪ BHAVA MAHĀSAMAYASATTVA ĀḤĀ.

The Tibetanized pronunciation of the Sanskrit mantra is:

OM BADZARSATTOSAMAYA MANUPALAYA BADZARSATTOTENOPA-TEETHA DRIDHROMEBHAVA SUTOKHAYOMEBHAVA SUPOKHA-YOMEBHAVA ANURAKTOMEBHAVA SARVASIDDHIMEPRAYATSTSHA SARVAKARMA SUTSAME TSITTAMSHRIYAMKURU HUNGHAHAHA-HAHO BHAGAWAN SARVATATHAGATA BADZAR MAMEMUNTSA BADZARBHAVA MAHASAMAYA SATTO AH.

6. This mantra is for purifying the phenomenal existents into emptiness.
In Sanskrit:

OṂ SVABHĀVAŚUDDHĀḤ-SARVADHARMĀḤ SVABHĀVASUDDHO 'HAM.

In Tibetan the pronunciation of the Sanskrit mantra is:

OM SOBHAVASHUDO SARVADHARMA SOBHAVASHUDO HANG.

7. See n. 2.
8. KLZ 38a/5: One day Noble Katyāyana, an adept disciple of the Buddha, approached a house for alms. There he saw the master of the household holding a baby in his lap, eating a fish, and beating a dog who came to grab a bone of the fish. When the Noble One examined their past lives through his omniscient power, he realized that the fish was the rebirth of the master's father and the dog was the rebirth of his mother in his present life and the baby was the rebirth of the enemy who had killed him in his last life. At this he said:

> Eating father's meat, beating mother,
> Holding in his lap the enemy who murdered him,
> And the wife eating the bone of her husband—
> The way of saṃsāra makes me laugh!

9. It is the Dhāraṇi of Akṣobhya Buddha.
In Sanskrit:

NAMO RATNATRAYĀYA OṂ KAṂKANIKAṂKANI ROCANIROCANI TROṬANITROṬANI TRĀSANITRĀSANI PRATIHANAPRATIHANA SARVAKARMAPARAMPARA ṆIME SARVASATTVANĀÑCA SVĀHĀ.

The Tibetan pronunciation of the Sanskrit dhāraṇī:

NAMO-RATNATYAYAYA OM KANKANIKANKANI ROTSANIROTSANI TROTANITROTANI TRASANITRASANI PRATIHANAPRATIHANA SARVAKARMAPARAMPARANIME SARVASATTONANTSASOHA.

10. OṂ BHRŪṂ SVĀHĀ. OṂ AMṚTĀYURDADE SVĀHĀ.
11. AH A HA ŚA SA MA.
12. *dKyil-'Khor gSum.* The three maṇḍalas of the three seats. (See note 13).
13. *gDan-gSum*: According to GDN 29b/6, the maṇḍalas of the three seats are the maṇḍalas of Male and Female Thus-gones (Buddhas), the maṇḍala of Male and Female Bodhisattvas, and the maṇḍala of Male and Female Wrathful Deities. The purified form or the purity of one's fivefold aggregates (*Phung-Po*) are the five Male Buddhas, and the purity of the five elements (*Khams* or *'Byung-Ba*) are the five Female Buddhas. The purity of one's sense faculties (*sKye-mCh'ed*), the four right and four left side senses and their sense-objects, are the eight Male and the eight Female Bodhisattvas. The purity of the sense of body, the sense faculty of body and the feeling and touch awareness of the four parts or limbs of the body, are the four Wrathful Door Protectors; and the purity of the four extremes are the four Wrathful Female Door Protectors.
14. *Dam-Pa Rigs-brGya*: This refers to the forty-two peaceful deities and fifty-eight wrathful deities.
15. The chief wrathful deity at the center of the maṇḍala.
16. *Tshogs-brGyad Kauri-Ma brGyad*: These are eight out of the twenty Wrathful Female Retinue Deities of the maṇḍala of the Hundred Peaceful and Wrathful Deities. According to PCM 327b/2, these eight are also known as *gNas-Kyi Ma-Mo brGyad,* the Eight Signs or symbols of the purity of the eight consciousnesses, the Sources of saṃsāra. According to GDN 44a/4, the female deity representing the purity of the universal basis is Gaurī (*dKar-Mo*), of mind consciousness is Caurī (*Ch'om-rKun-Ma*), of defiled mind is Pramohā (*Rab-rMong-Ma*), of consciousness of body is Vetali (*Ro-Lang-Ma*), of consciousness of eye is Caṇḍālī (*gTum-Mo*), of consciousness of nose is Pukkasī (*sPos-Ma*), of consciousness of tongue is Ghosmarī (*sMe-Sha-Chan*), and of consciousness of ear is Śmaśānā (*Dur-Khrod-Ma*).
17. *Yul-brGyad Phra-Men-Ma* (or *Phyag-rGya*) *brGyad*: These are eight out of the twenty Wrathful Female Retinue Deities of the maṇḍala of the Hundred Peaceful and Wrathful Deities. According to PCM 327b/5, they are the eight signs or symbols of the purity of the eight objects of the eight consciousnesses. According to GDN 44b/3, the female deity representing the purity of the object of the universal basis is *Seng-gDong-Ma,* of the object of mind conscious-

ness is *sTag-gDong-Ma,* of the object of defiled mind is *Wa-gDong-Ma,* of the object of touch is *sPyang-gDong-Ma,* of the object of sight is *Bya-rGod gDong-Ma,* of the object of smell is *Dur-Bya-gDong-Ma,* of the object of taste is *Bya-Rog gDong-Ma,* and of the object of sound is *A'ug-gDong-Ma.*

18. According to GDN 45a/2, the female deity representing the purity of the extreme view of eternalism is *lChags-Kyu-Ma,* of nihilism is *Zhags-Pa-Ma,* of self/ego is *sChags-sGrog-Ma,* and of characteristics is *Dril-Bu-Ma.*
19. The twenty-eight Lords are as follows: The six of the east are *Srin-Mo, Tshangs-Pa, Lha-Ch'en, rTogs-'Dod-Ma, gZhon-Nu-Ma,* and *brGya-Byin.* The six of the south are *rDo-rJe-Ma, bDud-rTsi-Ma, Zla-Ba, Be-Chon-Ma, Sri-Mo-Ma,* and *Za-Ba.* The six of the west are *dGa'-Ba, sTobs-Ch'en, rDo-rJe, 'Dod-Pa, Nor-Srung-Ma,* and *rLung-Lha.* The six of the north are *gSod-Byed, Me-Mo, Phag-Mo, rGan-Byed-Ma, sNa-Ch'en-Ma,* and *Ch'u-Lha.* The four door protectors are *rDo-rJe Nag-Mo, rDo-rJe Ser-Nag, rDo-rJe dMar-Nag,* and *rDo-rJe lJang-Nag.*
20. According to NGJ 30b, the ten Wrathful Male Deities of the Vajrakīla maṇḍala correspond to the following ten virtuous deeds: *rNam-Par rGyal-Ba* is for purification or the purity (or pure nature) of anger, *gShin-rJe gShed-Po* of pride, *rTa-mGrin rGyal-Po* of desire, *bDud-rTsi 'Khyil-Ba* of jealousy, *sTobs-Po-Ch'e* of ignorance, *dByug-Pa sNgon-Po* of lying, *Mi-gYo MGon-Po* of killing, *gZhan-Mi-Thub* of stealing, *Khams-gSum rNam-rGyal* of ill will, and *Hūṃkāra* of wrong view.
21. I couldn't find in Jigme Lingpa's writings how the ten virtuous deeds correspond to the ten Wrathful Female Deities. However, from his presentation, quoted in note 20, of how the ten Wrathful Male Deities correspond to the ten nonvirtuous deeds, it is clear which Wrathful Female Deities correspond to which of the ten virtuous deeds. The ten Wrathful Female Deities are the consorts of the ten Wrathful Male Deities and the ten virtuous deeds are the absence of the ten nonvirtuous deeds. *rDo-rJe sNyem-Ma* is the purity (or pure nature) of no-anger, *Dur-Khrod bDag-Mo* of no-pride, *rDo-rJe gTum-Mo* of no-desire, *rDo-rJe rLung-'Byin* of no-jealousy, *rDo-rJe bsKyod-Ma* of no-ignorance, *rDo-rJe sDer-Mo* of no-lying, *rDo-rJe gTun-Kung* of no-killing, *rDo-rJe mDa'-sNyems-Ma* of no-stealing, *rDo-rJe gSod-Ma* of no-ill-will, and *Hūṃkāra* of no-wrong-view.
22. *Ging-Ch'en bCho-brGyad:* According to GDN 90a/5, *Ging* (or Kiṅ-

kara) is the synonym for *Pho-Nya,* i. e., deputy, messenger, or courier. The eighteen Deputies are: nine male consorts including *rDo-rJe gNod-sByin* and *rDo-rJe sPyang-Ki,* and nine female consorts including *rDo-rJe 'Khrul-Mo-Ch'e* and *rDo-rJe Ging-rTsam.*

23. *Pho-Nya Sum-brGya Drug-Chu:* these are the six divisions of sixty deities such as *rDo-rJe 'Bar-Ba* and *mThong-Byed-Ma.*
24. *dBang-Po'i sGo bDun Ma-Mo bDun. Mamo Gangshar,* DC 12a/6, gives seven Ma (or Mamo) as part of the twenty-eight retinues of the *Ma-Mo rBod-gTong* maṇḍala. They are *Kun-Grags, Kun-bZang, Grags-sNyems Kun-sGrol, rDo-rJe Ye-Shes mCh'og, rDo-rJe A'od-Ch'ags, rDo-rJe gSal-Phro,* and *gYu-sGron.* I am not sure what the seven doors of faculties are (*dBang-Po'i sGo*), nor do I know how the seven Mamos correspond to the seven doors of faculties. Nevertheless, according to NA 70b/6 and BGT-II 1933, the seven basis faculties (*rTen Gyi dBang-Po*) are the faculties of eye, ear, nose, tongue, body, mind, and life (*Srog*). However, these seven doors of faculties seem different from what we are looking for. The empowerment text of Gangshar says (DR 23a/3): "Having dissolved the seven wisdom sisters into the seven consciousnesses of the disciple, the seven consciousnesses are purified." According to SC-I, 85, 86a/5, the seven consciousnesses are the consciousnesses of eye, ear, nose, tongue, body, mind, and defiled mind.
25. *bsTan-Ma bChu-gNyis:* the twelve female land protectors of Tibet known as Tenma are *Tshe-Ring-Ma, rDo-rJe Ya-Ma-sKyong, Kun-bZang-Mo, bGegs-Kyi gTso, sPyan-gChig-Ma, mKha'-lDing Klu-Mo, rDo-rJe Khyung-bTsun-Ma, Drag-Mo rGyal, Bod-Khams sKyong, rDo-rJe sMan gChig-Ma, gYar-Mo bSil,* and *rDo-rJe Zu-Le sMan.*
26. *'Dod-Yon Gyi Lha-Mo lNga:* the offering goddesses of the five sensory objects: form, sound, smell, taste, and touch.
27. *dBang-bZhi:* the empowerments of vase, secret, wisdom, and words.
28. *'Phrog-Ma:* There is a story in the Buddhist scriptures that there was a female nonhuman spirit with five hundred sons who lived by eating babies whom they stole. Then in the presence of the Buddha they renounced their evil activities, and in return the Buddha advised his monk disciples to dedicate their merit and leftover meals to them. Even today, in the Tibetan Buddhist tradition, with special prayers the monks give the last part of their meals to Hārītī and her sons.